OLD STONE WALLS

Also by Norman J. Van Valkenburgh

Non-fiction

The Adirondack Forest Preserve: A Chronology

Land Acquisition for New York State: An Historical Perspective

On the Adirondack Survey with Verplank Colvin:
The Diaries of Percy Reese Morgan
(Edited and with additional material)

The Forest Preserve of New York State
in the Adirondack and Catskill Mountains

Fiction

Murder in the Catskills

Mayhem in the Catskills

Mischief in the Catskills

Murder in the Shawangunks

For children

Cub Scouts Climb the Tower

OLD STONE WALLS
Catskill Land and Lore

Norman J. Van Valkenburgh

PURPLE MOUNTAIN PRESS
Fleischmanns, New York

Old Stone Walls: Catskill Land and Lore

First edition 2004

Published by Purple Mountain Press, Ltd.
1060 Main Street, P.O. Box 309
Fleischmanns, New York 12430-0309
845-254-4062, 845-254-4476 (fax), purple@catskill.net
http://www.catskill.net/purple

Parts of this book appeared previously in other publications for which grateful acknowledgment is made on pages 111-112.

ISBN 1-930098-55-3
Library of Congress Control Number: 2004104046

Cover painting: *Spring, Palmer Hill* by John Hopkins
Cover typography: Hinterland Design, Coxsackie, NY

Manufactured in the United States of America.
Printed on acid-free paper.

For Andrew

May his life be full of adventures
and his eyes sparkle with anticipation
as he embarks on each one.

CONTENTS

INTRODUCTION

WE LAND SURVEYORS can agree with William Parsons (1701-1757), an early Pennsylvania practitioner, who described our profession as "a Business Some Times a little profitable but on the other hand of continual Trouble and Disquietude."

It's safe to conclude that God was one of the first surveyors—if not the very first. When Amos saw Him standing "upon a wall made by a plumbline, with a plumbline in his hand" (Amos 7:7), He was obviously engaged in measuring a shot down the wall. Since God was the one with the plumb bob, He was certainly the head chainman. Amos doesn't record who the rear chainman was; maybe Moses, Gabriel, Joshua, or some other lesser light. Perhaps Methuselah; after all, surveyors are said to lead long lives.

Those who now measure distances electronically probably wouldn't know what to do with all the impedimenta chainmen once had to contend with. Thankfully, one no longer has to use plumb bobs, hand levels, chaining pins, spring balances, and the like to get an accurate measurement.

Men of stature, in addition to God, are known to surveying history. George Washington started out as a surveyor and ended up being "Father of His Country." It is said that Abraham Lincoln ran out a survey or two. The names of Charles Mason and Jeremiah Dixon live on in the line they laid down in 1763-67 between Pennsylvania and Maryland. Meriwether Lewis and William Clark spent nearly two years (1804-05) running a line from St. Louis westerly across the Rocky Mountains to the mouth of the Columbia River on the Pacific Shore.

Here in the Catskill Mountains and the Lower Hudson Valley

we carry on the legacy of early predecessors who left their marks on the countryside. Probably the first were the Brothers Wooster who ran the outbounds (or most of it anyway) of the great Hardenburgh Patent, all 1.5-million acres of it. The records aren't quite sure which brother, Ebeneezer or Henry, ran which line of the patent; now and then it's recorded simply that such and such line was run by "one Worster, the Surveyor." Once the Livingstons had acquired the major share of the patent, their surveyor, William Cockburn, subdivided it for them. The Livingstons were long on land and short on cash (actually they hated to part with it) and sometimes compensated Will with the first rather than the latter. Thus Will ended up owning so-called "Expense Lots" all over the Catskills. Others, Christopher Tappan, James Cockburn (William's son), John Cox, Alexander Daniels, and Jonas Smith among them, had a hand in running boundary lines in and around the patent in the late 1700s and early 1800s.

Yet today, surveyors deep in the woods cannot fail to recognize a John B. Davis corner when they run onto one. John's corners were imposing, usually consisting of a slabbed center stone three, four, or more feet high with huge stones piled around it. Even the legendary Verplanck Colvin came out of the hallowed Adirondacks in 1898 for a visit to the Catskills. He did no surveys; after interviewing a couple of local surveyors, he headed back north. Speculation was he had come to find out how real surveyors did it.

Down in Kingston town and its environs, Edward B. Codwise held the high ground in the early years of the last century. It has been said that no other surveyor or anyone carrying a transit was allowed within the city limits. The story goes that he was seen in the field only when some question was raised by one of his crews about where to set a critical corner. Then he would appear on site wearing his characteristic bowler hat and frock coat, look over the surroundings, peer this way and that, authoritatively point to a spot on the ground and say, "The corner is right there." His clients thought him marvelous and endowed with some sort of sixth sense no other surveyor had or could ever hope to have. Actually, it was just that the cost of the survey was nearing the original estimate and it was time to finish it up and get on to the next one.

When surveyors move off the flatlands and head for the hills they are likely to follow the "tracks" of Ed West. His career spanned the mid-Twentieth Century. From 1920 and on into 1988, he climbed every peak of the Catskills, explored every clove known to man and some that weren't, looked over every valley and draw big enough to hold a mountain brook, and tried to teach the surveyor's craft to every young lad who showed an interest in it.

I have no illusions I have left any blazes on the landscape that will measure up (Yes, pun intended) to all those icons who came before me. Still, some of my moments in time have seemed worthy enough to be set down for others to read. If surveyors and laymen don't find enough in the pages of this book to hold their interest, perhaps my great-grandson will when he becomes old enough to wonder just what it was his aged relative did with his life.

Note: Some of the essays and/or articles herein were previously published elsewhere in a slightly different form, many in a biweekly column, "Catskill Parkways," I wrote from 1995 through 2000 for *The Mountain Eagle*, a weekly newspaper with editorial offices at Tannersville, New York. Acknowledgment has been made in every case of an earlier publication at the end of this book.

PEOPLE, PLACES, AND THINGS

THOSE OF US who work mostly on wildland surveys seldom see anyone other than those on our crew of the day. Now and then we run into another surveyor who is as lost (but only for the moment) as we are, and it's not unusual to see a lumberman once in a while or the occasional hiker. I once enountered a topless hiker on an old woods road out in the middle of nowhere. She didn't notice me until we were about twenty feet apart, although I had spotted her long before that. I tipped my cap with a "Good afternoon." She wished me the same but didn't tip anything. We passed and went our separate ways without looking back. After all, bare backs aren't that uncommon.

Given their trade, lumbermen tend to be loners and more irascible than most. The ones with less than a sterling reputation are irresistibly drawn to the fine timber stands on the state land next to the private land where they are working. Wolfgang H. was one of those, and we once got him on a major trespass. After we had surveyed the line (a bigger job than it should have been because the old blazed line trees had been cut and hauled off to the mill) and counted the stumps on the state land side, Ed decided we should stop in at Wolfgang's cabin and confront him with what we had found.

Wolfgang lived in the last place on a dead-end road which turned into dirt a mile or so before we got there. The front yard (well, it wasn't really a yard) was aclutter with a couple of battered trucks, a derelict bulldozer, a pile of rotting hemlock logs (the market for hemlock had faded long ago), and a heap of maple chunks waiting to be split for firewood. A couple of rangy German shepherds growled a greeting as they lunged at the ends of their chains, which were—fortunately—anchored to iron truck axels driven into the ground. As Ed approached the house (the rest of us decided we could better offer moral support while sitting in the car), the door opened and there stood Wolfgang, who was not a pretty sight even in his better moments. This was not one of them. His full black beard bristled, his hair looked like it hadn't felt—or even seen—a comb in days; his plaid shirt was open halfway down revealing a massive, hairy (black, too) chest, and his forearms bulged beneath rolled-up sleeves. What really got our attention (and Ed's, too) was the rifle he held cradled in his left arm. "Who are you, and what do you want?" he asked.

We didn't hear Ed's answer, but it didn't take long. He was muttering to himself as he returned to the car, "Guess we'll let the enforcement people take care of this one." Seemed like a wise decision to me.

Lew H. was another Catskills' lumberman who wasn't much deterred by blazed boundary lines, especially those marking the state lands. Lew always paid the minimal fines set by law but was heard to say time and again, "Cheapest timber I can find is on state land." It got to be kind of a joke. Finally, the Department of Law decided something drastic had to be done. After a particularly egregious trespass, the lawyers charged Lew with grand larceny. It worked. The court levied such a high fine that Lew had to liquidate his business, sawmill and all, to pay it.

At the other end of the legal matrix was Bill B. Whenever we found a questionable title to a piece of state land, the Department of Law assigned the problem to Bill to sort out. That meant Bill had to come down from Albany to look over the information turned up by our research. He always showed up just before noon and then had to go out for lunch, which usually extended well into the afternoon. By then it was nearly time to head back to Albany which meant any deep discussion of the issue had to be put off till another day.

Bill was a bit of a dandy. He always came dressed in his best lawyering outfit—dark suit, white shirt, conservative tie, shined shoes—he hardly fit in with us low-paid, survey-laborer types. He usually handled everything with a long-winded discussion—once he got down to it that is.

It came as a complete surprise to us when he once said he wanted to look at the questionable parcel on the ground. Ed told him beforehand it was on the back side of a low boggy area, beyond a fringe of blackberry bushes, and that the black flies were in season. No matter, Bill wanted to see it anyway.

Well, he came, dressed to the nines as usual. To make it even more ludicrous, he brought his wife, who we hadn't met before, and she was dressed in a frilly summer dress, hair beautifully coifed, and wearing high heels. Ed took one look at the two of them and said, "Guess you decided not to look at the parcel."

"Oh, no," Bill and his wife replied in unison, "We've been planning this for some time."

So they went. We didn't see them when they returned, but Ed told us they didn't look quite the same as when they had arrived. Bill never again suggested he wanted to see any state land parcels. And that was the only time we ever saw Bill's wife.

Some of the pieces that make up this section tell the stories of some other people I ran into over the years while surveying their lands or properties nearby. Others describe places I have been and some of the sights I have seen on my journeys.

OLD STONE WALLS

LOOKING ACROSS TO THE CATSKILLS from the middle of the Kingston-Rhinecliff Bridge, one has to wonder just what possessed the early settlers to pass by the productive lowlands for the harsh environment of the foreboding mountains. This puzzle becomes more perplexing when these hills are capped with snow and being savaged by the wild winds of winter.

The mountains rear up from the plains like giants, creating their own horizon; the only way to scale them (from the east anyway) was to climb up through craggy cloves that had been carved over the millennia by swift, plunging, ice-cold streams. Whatever prompted these staunch individuals, they came and sought out the upper reaches of the deep valleys hemmed in by steep slopes. These seemed to have been built in layers with distinct levels of ledges and outcroppings of rock that only added to the desolateness of the landscape. Were these people running from something and seeking some kind of sanctuary or hiding place? Or were they simply unsociable types looking for a quiet place far off the beaten path? No matter what their purpose, they turned out to be as rugged as their surroundings. They had to be in order to scrape a living—and a meager one it must have been—from a coarse soil suited only to growing rock and thorn apple and not much else. Why ever they came, they found an inexhaustible supply of building material.

Alf Evers, in his colossal *The Catskills: From Wilderness to Woodstock*, relates the answer he got when he asked an old-timer how he could tell just where the Catskills began—"You keep on going until you get to where there's two stones to every dirt. Then, b' Jesus, you're there."

Indeed, few would argue with that interpretation. One of the better-forgotten memories of my youth on the family farm is of picking stones from the garden plot on the hill in back of the house. As soon as the snow melted and the ground dried, I picked what must have been tons of stones so the soil—what there was of it—could be plowed and dragged prior to planting. That, of course, turned up other stones and I started on another round of the same thing. With the job done, I expected next spring would find the ground clear. Not so. During the winter, a whole new crop of stones grew; I never knew how, but there they were.

The task of the first farmers was more monumental. They had to remove trees, brush, and brambles from flats and hillsides so they could pasture livestock and plant crops, but this only exposed acres of rock and stone that also had to be cleared. They soon realized here was the raw material with which they could build walls to divide one ownership from another, pastures from home sites, fields from wood lots, and foundations for houses, barns, wagon sheds, and the all-important outhouses.

Robert Frost, in his delightful "Mending Wall," wrote, "Good fences make good neighbors." Surveyors know that stone walls do the job best of all.

Those who built the first stone walls must have followed close behind the surveyors who laid out the original patents, tracts, and lots. If not, how come great lot lines reaching up and over the ridges of the Catskills are marked by stone walls exactly in range from one valley to the next? They run down the lower slopes of one mountain, cross the bottom land, climb halfway up the next mountain straight as an arrow, and appear again on the other side directly in line.

Stone walls are holy relics to surveyors; nothing better marks where one property ends and the next begins. Perhaps this reverence derives from knowing the very first builder of walls. Amos tells of seeing the Lord standing "upon a wall made by a plumbline, with a plumbline in his hand." The obvious question is, was the Lord simply the stone mason who built the wall or the surveyor who laid it out? Or both?

My grandfather told me how walls came to be so straight. The early stone masons were also fond of drink, he said. The farmers who hired them marked the point where the wall was to begin and then set a bottle of whiskey out ahead at a distance marking the end of a day's work. The mason could have the bottle when he reached it, so he took the straightest line in order to get there the quickest. And that's why straight walls were called whiskey walls, my grandfather explained. Perhaps crooked walls were constructed by those who started the day where the bottle was set instead of at the other end.

However, surveyors must be cautious before accepting a stone wall as marking a certain line as I learned early on in my apprenticeship with the master of Catskill Mountain surveyors. Coming upon a well-built wall tracking across the steep side hill and disappearing into the woods, I remarked, "That looks like a lot line to me." Not one to suffer fools, Ed snorted, "It's a lot line all right, between the sheep lot and the cow lot." We moved on, not giving that wall a second glance.

The argument could easily be made that stone walls are works of art. Not only do they have utility, they have grace and beauty as well. Some have fallen, collapsed from age and neglect, but still trace a painter's brush stroke across the landscape. Others are as solid as the day they were built and mark out huge checkerboards on green summer hills and winter countrysides. Those wandering around remote cellar holes and old barn foundations stitch a crazy-quilt portrait of a forgotten family who once lived and labored there.

Maybe those rugged individuals who first settled these mountains had a bit of the artist in their souls. The stone walls they left behind seem to say so.

THE FARMER AND HIS WIFE

THOSE who take up the land surveyors' trade in New York's Catskill Mountains are destined to see parts of the countryside where others have ne'er or rarely been. Unlike the hiker who walks the beaten path and the deer hunter who sits or stands in one place most of the day, the surveyor travels the straight line through rock-strewn gullies, knee-deep bogs, and never-ending (so it seems) stretches of brambles, briars, and mountain laurel. However, he is rewarded with sights of hidden waterfalls, wide vistas from hard-won mountain tops, long-lost glens of massive hemlocks missed by the tanners, yellow lady slippers nodding in the breeze, and swirling snow blocking the view to everywhere.

The farmer's wife was frantic when she reached me by telephone. The local real estate broker had put a FOR SALE sign in the middle of their upper pasture, she said, the one next to the town road. He had refused her requests to take it down, telling them his surveyor said it was part of the adjoining property which he now owned. He was subdividing that into lots, and this was the prime one, he told her. They couldn't afford to have the whole farm surveyed, she said, but could I help them get their land back? Her husband's family had farmed the place, including that lot, for three generations; didn't that count for something?

As it was, I had planned a trip to the county clerk's office in a week or so to research another survey so said I would look up the deeds for their farm and the next-door property while I was there. When I came back through that day, I would look at the lot and then stop at their home to tell them what I found. Her voice in reply sounded relieved. Between times, I went to the state office and picked up aerial photographs of the area including the farm and adjoining lands.

The deeds were pretty straightforward. Although both properties were made up of a number of separate parcels, each was well-described by bearings, distances, and acreages. These were easy to trace out on the aerials, which clearly showed stone walls and hedgerows marking the lines of each parcel. Since I hadn't been on the ground, I wasn't sure which part of the farm had been claimed by the broker's surveyor but found out soon enough.

My helper and I drove up the town road past the farmhouse and just over the brow of the hill saw a large sign nailed to a wooden post set in the middle of an attractive, flat, cleared lot of about 10 acres announcing it to be FOR SALE. It was, indeed, part of the farm, being the third parcel in the deed and had been purchased by the farmer's grandfather in the mid-1800s. We walked around it with a compass and dragging a chain to verify the deed description. We couldn't understand how the surveyor had made such an error. On the other hand, I knew the surveyor; he wasn't one. He hadn't been able to meet the requirements to become licensed but practiced anyway. It was the real estate broker and others like him who kept him in business.

We went to the farmhouse where the old couple were waiting for us. They were, of course, delighted with our report. I suggested they call the broker and ask him to come down so I could explain the correct location of the boundary line between the properties. As his wife hung up from the call, the farmer said to her, "Better call Bill. He wouldn't want to miss this."

I didn't know who Bill was but soon learned that he was the neighbor across the road and had once had a run-in with the same surveyor. No sooner had the second call been made when, looking out the window, I saw Bill scampering across the road pulling on his jacket as he hurried along.

It wasn't long before the broker drove in. He and I and my helper sat around the dining room table so we could spread out the aerial photographs and deeds as we talked. The farmer was in his big rocking chair off to one side, filling his pipe. His wife was in the kitchen; I could hear the sounds of pots and pans and bowls and wooden spoons and something bubbling on the stove. Bill sat in a straight-backed chair in a far corner of the room. He hadn't said anything since arriving.

It didn't take long to convince the broker of the error of his survey. He understood the terms in the deed and agreed with my plotting of them on the photos. He pulled back his chair and said, "I'll call my surveyor and get him over here. You can run through this again for his benefit."

The surveyor came—reluctantly I could tell as he walked in the door and took a seat at the table. The farmer leaned back in his chair and contentedly blew great clouds of smoke toward the ceiling. His wife emerged from the kitchen carrying a tray filled with steaming cups of coffee and a plate piled high with freshly-made donuts.

The surveyor was silent as I went through the deeds and pointed out the lines of each parcel on the aerial photographs. He remained unconvinced as I neared the end saying only, "You can't scale on aerial photographs."

Bill finally spoke, not loud enough for anyone to hear, but I sat facing him and could make out his words as he looked at me. "Get him," he said. "Go get him," over and over again.

The surveyor left still not admitting his error; however, the broker said he would stop at the pasture lot and remove the sign. It was obviously part of the farm, he said, and apologized to the farmer and his wife for the trouble he had caused and, "Oh, yes," could he "have another doughnut or two to take along."

My helper and I also made ready to leave. The farmer reached for his wallet and wanted to know how much they owed us. I said not to worry about it right then; I would send a bill later. I didn't but wrote them a letter saying I was making no charge for such a delightful afternoon and those delicious doughnuts. Nevertheless, a check arrived by return mail. It wasn't a great amount, still probably more than they could afford, but satisfied their need to settle a debt.

I was more than amply paid, however. The real estate broker decided it was time to get a different surveyor, and when he did, I got to see parts of the Catskills I might otherwise have missed.

LOGGERS AND THE RUSTIC

AMONG THE PLEASURES experienced by land surveyors are people met along the way and the interesting situations one becomes part of from time to time. While rummaging through some old files, I was reminded of a few.

One happened just a couple of months after I was licensed to practice. Practice? Hell, too; I wasn't going to practice, I was going out there and do it. This milestone in life was reached after a six-year apprenticeship with the doyen of Catskill Mountain surveyors, uncounted hours of study night after night over the preceding two years, and a grueling eight-hour examination I thought I had failed but didn't. I was pretty proud of myself and more than a little overwhelmed with my own importance. It's a wonder I didn't hang a sign around my neck announcing my brand new license to the world.

My helper and I were up the north side of the Spruceton Valley running a traverse along the lines of state lands near the top of that mountain range. About mid-afternoon we came upon two loggers sitting on some rocks beside an old woods road, their chain saws silent for the moment. They were obviously at work cutting timber on the adjoining private land. Their experience stood out in the weather-beaten lines that creased their faces and the rough clothes and battered, but rugged, boots they wore. The finely-honed teeth of their chain saws and the razor-sharp ax carefully propped beside one of the men left no doubt they knew their business.

As an emissary of the state charged with protecting its lands and wanting to impress the men with my authority, I hauled a number of old maps from my pack and spread them out on the ground before them. I then launched into a long-winded lecture about how they should pay attention to the boundary lines we were marking and not stray beyond them and cut any of the state's trees. I waved my arms this way and that up the blazed line and, using a stick as a pointer, indicated it on the old survey maps. The loggers were quiet throughout, hanging onto my every word I thought.

Well-satisfied after about ten minutes that I had fully enlightened them on the subjects of surveying, the sanctity of the state land, and just who I was, I folded the maps and stuffed them back into my pack. Seeing I had finished, the two men got up.

"Can't hear a word you say," said the one obviously in charge, "Deaf." I later found out the two were brothers in a family in which many of the male members were deaf. They had hearing aids but didn't wear them in the woods to cut down the noise of the chain saws.

They picked up their saws and the ax and headed down the mountain without a backward glance. My helper, suppressing a laugh with some difficulty, started up the line. I just stood there, vowing that would be the first and only lecture I would deliver to loggers encountered in the woods—or anywhere else for that matter.

ED AND I WERE PERPLEXED. In the early years of my career (some will say yet), I could be perplexed quite easily but Ed never was. We had a copy of the deed by which the parcel had been parted off the farm some years before, but nothing seemed to fit. The point of beginning was well-described—" a large maple tree standing on the side of the road just northerly of the old barn"—and we had no trouble finding that. However, when we traversed from it on the cited bearing and measured the deed distance with our 1-chain (66 feet), steel tape, we overshot the first corner—or what we suspected was the first corner. We continued on, laying out the bearings and distances called for in the deed. With each leg of the traverse, we seemed to be farther and farther away from what we thought were the corners described by the deed. The final course brought us back to the maple tree all right, but the 50-acre parcel we were supposed to have turned out to be nearly 70 acres the way we had it.

Ed was really puzzled by this time and that was out of the ordinary. "Let's go talk to Marion," he decided. Marion was the old widower who lived alone in the ramshackle farmhouse across from the barn. "He's the one who sold off the 50 acres. He can tell us who did the survey," Ed reasoned.

Well, Marion could. In fact, he and that "city feller" who bought the 50 acres laid out the parcel themselves.

"How'd you measure the lines?" Ed asked.

"With a rope," Marion snorted. "We measured out a chain, tied a knot to mark it, and counted up the number of knots as we went."

"How long is a chain?" Ed inquired.

Marion was quick to reply. "Fifty feet," he snapped. "Any damn fool knows that."

"Ah, yes," Ed acknowledged, sagely nodding his head.

We went across the road to the maple tree and started the traverse again. When we multiplied the number of chains given for each course by 50 feet instead of 66 feet as we had been doing, it all fit—or, reasonably so—and we ended up back at the maple tree with a 50-acre parcel.

Oddly enough, I ran into this same measurement conversion years later. While traversing the centerline of a long-abandoned town road using the description by which it had originally been dedicated, I missed each bend in the road by quite a few feet. As I stood there trying to figure out what was wrong, I remembered Marion's chain. Sure enough, when I used 50 feet instead of 66 to convert the deed distances over to feet, the old description matched every bend on the ground. I wondered if one of Marion's forebears had surveyed that road when it had been laid out many years before.

THE COLLECTOR

JOHN B. was a collector; however, he wasn't interested in the usual stamps, coins, old books, etc, sought by others. John collected stuff. He didn't much care what it was as long as it took up space. John apparently had an aversion to emptiness and was hell-bent to fill it up.

The area (I hesitate to use the word lawn) around the house was piled with stacks of rotting lumber, rusty remains of old farm machinery, the broken frame of a hay rigging, a washing machine or two, the chassis of at least one vintage automobile, and all sorts of other useless odds and ends. Corridors had been kept open where sidewalks led to the house and on up the hill to the barn. Another gap had been left next to the road so John could pull in and park his old, brown, pickup truck. When it was there, newcomers to the valley weren't sure if it was in current use or just part of the landscape. The right front fender wobbled at speeds over ten miles an hour but was held in place by strands of barbed wire. The front bumper was tied on with a piece of rope. The tailboard had rusted through and fallen off long ago but had been saved on one pile or another—John wasn't sure which one. Nevertheless, the truck ran just fine and carried John and Bird (short for Bertha) down to the village to do their trading and farther afield so John could pick up items to add to his collection.

I don't think John ever bought any of the things he stored around the place. Most folks were happy to have him take away what they might have called junk but which turned out to be just what John was looking for at the moment. He never sold anything either. As best anyone could tell, he didn't have too many pieces worth buying anyway.

John never smiled; he was a morose man with a perpetual

scowl on his face. He wore bib overalls and walked bent over at the shoulders, head forward, as if scanning the ground looking for something.

Bird was a contrast. She was a jovial sort with a smile for everyone she met. She was a round, sprightly lady, who fancied the same ensemble as John; that is, she too wore bib overalls. She was genuinely liked by all and was more cosmopolitan that most people knew. This was best illustrated by an anecdote told by her doctor. She lived her final few days in the old Margaretville Hospital. She knew her time was short as did Dr.Palen. He asked on one of his rounds near the last if he could get anything for her.

"Yes," she replied, "I'd like a Tom Collins." The doctor went down to the hotel on Main Street, ordered the drink complete with a cherry and an orange slice to go and took it back to Bird. He brought that treat to her every evening until the day she died.

Of all the sights at John's place, the one that drew the most attention was the wagon house across the road. It was smaller than the barn, although the second level had once been a hay mow. The ground floor was, of course, crammed full with broken-down farm machinery and other items of John's collection. The roof was missing quite a few shingles and boards now and then fell off one side or the other. As full as it was, the building still developed a decided lean and seemed sure to tip over entirely. Some talked of starting a pool with the winner being the one who picked the date when John's wagon shed finally collapsed. It never did. He just kept adding stuff to both floors until it was full to the roof. While that prevented the building from tipping altogether, the lean was never corrected and it stayed that way until later owners removed the stuff that held it up and disassembled it as it stood, lean and all.

The wagon shed had another curiosity not many noticed. It was five-sided. One back corner—the one farthest from the road—looked like it had been cut off. It wasn't; it had been built that way. The builder must have had some reason or purpose for that odd construction and I always wondered what it was. I found out when I surveyed the property after John and Bird passed on and the new owner wanted to know just what it was he had acquired.

The property line on that side of the road crossed the field at an angle parallel to and about one foot off the fifth side of the wagon shed with just enough room left for the roof overhang. The builder had apparently started to construct a normal, four-sided structure before realizing the back corner would extend over onto the adjoining property. Rather that shifting the foundation about five feet to clear the boundary—as most others would have done—the builder had, instead, cut off the offending corner and added a fifth side to the building to keep it on John's side of the line. I never knew who the builder was but suspect it was John's personal handiwork; it would have fit right in with his way of doing things.

It was kind of a shame the place got cleaned up. Local folks had gotten used to it and didn't consider it an eyesore. Visitors to the valley thought it a unique conversation piece. Some thought it could have made a great tourist attraction.

CHARACTERS

SIMILAR TO MANY RURAL NEIGHBORHOODS, the mountain-top regions of the Catskills have seen their share of characters. Some are long forgotten (and maybe just as well) but a few live on in stories handed down the generations with the admonition they not be told outside the family circle and to only a selected few within it.

When traveling the back country, surveyors also run into some eccentrics now and then and pick up a few stories of their own. These too get passed from one generation to the next and the characters in them take on life again as their tales are told.

Indeed, Harry W., who came from over Goshen Street way does seem destined to live forever. Time was when Harry had pretty much run out of credit at the grocery and dry goods stores within easy reach of home and was forced to travel farther afield. Eventually, he showed up at the corner store in West Kill. Although extremely reluctant to do so, Alden H., the storekeeper, finally agreed to extend credit on the basis of Harry's sworn statement. Well, not actually sworn on a stack of bibles or anything as formal as that but sworn nonetheless.

"Alden," he vowed, "if it's the last thing I do before I die, I'll pay every cent I owe you."

When Harry's obituary appeared in the weekly newspaper, Alden refused to believe it. "Harry's not dead," he said, "he still hasn't paid his store bill." Alden passed away years ago but Harry evidently lives on somewhere out in the countryside, presumedly where credit is easy to come by.

THE HIGH WATER a few years back supposedly broke all records. They might have been shattered in most places but certainly not up in the dead-end valley of Spruceton. I'm not sure exactly when the record there was set, but it must have been some time in the 1940s according to the way Bill S. told the story. Some folks said Bill just plain made up things while others agreed he tended to exaggeration now and then. A few (darned few) pointed out that no matter how many times Bill told one of his many tales it always came out the same, so maybe there was some truth in what he said.

Whenever this deluge was, it went on for days and the level of the West Kill kept rising and tearing away at the stream banks as it rampaged down the valley. Bill became quite concerned because his house was perched on a bluff overlooking the stream and he could see the ground washing away threatening to undermine it. He kept a close watch of the situation, standing on top of the bluff most hours of the day. Good thing he did or, like everyone else, he would have missed the submarine.

"Yessir," said Bill, "when the water got the highest, this submarine went by on it's way up the valley and must still be there because I didn't see it come back."

During every high water since, residents along the stream have waited for some sign of the submarine finally returning down the valley. It hasn't, so it must still be up there moored in some hidden backwater no one has yet found.

Bill was an accomplished hunter and usually came home with

his share of game. Once, as he tells it, he was drawing a bead on a twelve-point buck and slowly pulling the trigger when a huge black bear ambled into the line of fire and reared up on his hind legs. Fazed not a bit, Bill squeezed off the shot. The bullet went clean through the bear (killing it, of course), got the deer in a vital spot to drop it too, continued on to hit a squirrel sitting on a log, and then ricocheted off a rock to bring down a pheasant which, excited by all the commotion, had flown up out of the brush at the edge of the woods. Some called it a lucky shot but Bill said he had it all lined up before he pulled the trigger.

Not long after jet airplanes replaced those with rotary engines and propellers, Bill was tracking a deer out of the woods into an open field. Just as he shot the deer (another kill don't you know), a single-engine jet came over the mountain flying so low the back blast blew off Bill's hat. The jet pulled straight up and, in Bill's words, "Lit those afterburners scorching a streak right across the middle of that field, singed the hair off the deer and roasted it to a medium well. Got my buck, ready to eat, right there on the spot." It don't get no better than that.

NOW, about that anonymous filling station attendant. Long before today's multi-pump, self-service stations; in fact, soon after automobiles began to travel the dirt roads hereabouts, garages with one pump—maybe two—appeared. These were usually owned and tended by a single mechanic, who nearly always wore a beanie like Goober on "The Andy Griffith Show," carried a large dirty rag in the back pocket of his greasy pants, and could be depended on to do almost everything from patching tubes, changing tires, pumping gas, to cleaning windshields (generally with the dirty rag) and anything else pertaining to an automobile.

The story, often told with settings in New York's Adirondacks or the Green and White Mountains of New England, most likely took place in the Catskills, John Burroughs's home country. While it may be more apocryphal than not, it is partly based on actual events.

In January of 1913, Henry Ford, in appreciation for the pleasure he got from reading John's books, presented him with a brand new Model T. The two became good friends and included Thomas Edison and Harvey Firestone in their circle. The four did, indeed, take a number of motor trips throughout the mountains of the Northeast, but it was when they stopped for gas at a remote valley settlement where the story may depart from fact.

The owner of the gas station, a typical Catskills' native, didn't really care who his customers were as long as they paid cash.

Ford, trying to start a conversation, asked, "Know who I am? I'm Henry Ford; I built this car." Paying no attention, the attendant continued to pump gas.

Edison then introduced himself, "I'm Thomas Edison; I invented the electric lights on the car." Still not impressed, the station owner kept on pumping gas.

Firestone next spoke up. "I'm Harvey Firestone; I made the tires on the car."

The gas tank full by this time, the owner finally responded, "Yeah, and I suppose next you're gonna tell me the old guy with the white beard sittin' in the back seat is Santa Claus."

Who knows, maybe the garage man had something there. What better way for old St. Nick to find out who's naughty or nice than by traveling the country incognito in an open-air touring car with three prominent men of the day?

HARDLY A DAY PASSES that we are not reminded of the array of law enforcement surrounding us. We spot the trooper hidden behind a tree off the side of the highway, a patrol car from the sheriff's office drives by, the newspaper reports on a class of conservation officers and forest rangers being graduated from the training academy, the morning crowd at the coffee shop talks about the need to expand the town police force when the skiing season begins, and the security guards at the mall down the mountain seem to watch everyone—when they're not talking to the salesgirls, that is. Is this much protection really necessary? Time was when about all the constabulary we saw—or needed—was Oat J.

I never knew where Oat came from or what place he called

headquarters; he just showed up now and then. He wasn't a real policeman, but acted as if he was. He traveled from village to village on a bicycle, always wearing a vintage World War I, wide-brimmed, campaign hat and a military jacket much too large for his small frame. The legs of his pants were held tight around his ankles by large, black, metal clips so the cuffs wouldn't catch between the chain and sprocket of his bicycle.

Oat's self-appointed, official duty was directing traffic. He didn't have a regular schedule. When the urge struck him, he stationed himself in front of Bailey's store over in Lexington—or at some other busy highway intersection—and sorted out the comings and goings of all the cars passing by. Most drivers—even those from out of town—abided by his hand signals. The World War I hat demanded respect.

As far as I know, Oat wasn't paid for his police work. His compensation was the satisfaction of bringing order to highway intersections as the need arose. His main source of income came from selling *Grit* newspapers and Cloverine Salve as he pedaled from place to place on his bicycle.

Once in a while Oat handled things at the Spruceton Road junction in West Kill. Among other duties he stopped traffic whenever Egbert V. wanted to cross over from the Beech Ridge side. Egbert didn't drive a car; his vehicle was a wheelbarrow. He didn't ride in it, but pushed it to and from Hyatt's store every few days or so to do his tradin'.

Egbert was a rotund man, the result of his particular fondness for beer. His wife had laid down the law more than once and, in their later years, believed she had kept him away from the brew—or it from him as the case may be. Egbert didn't drink anymore, she said, since she banned beer from the house. The neighbor ladies just nodded their heads; they knew about Egbert's trips to the store. Three miles down the Ridge it was, and three miles back—uphill most of the return journey.

Problem was, the tavern was just up the road from the grocery store and Egbert passed it both ways. The wheelbarrow was empty on the way off the Ridge except for an old hooked rug he brought along to put over his groceries to keep the sun off when he returned home. That's what he told his wife anyway. Actually it was to cover the bottles of beer he planned to buy. His wife never suspected he squirreled away some of the egg money so he could afford these extra purchases.

The tavern was Egbert's first stop. His timing was uncanny; he arrived at the door just as Mr. Flick was opening up for the day's business. Egbert stayed just long enough to drink one glass of beer and buy a quart bottle to take along. This was tucked under the rug out of sight from the curious. Fortunately, the road between the tavern and the store was shaded by some large trees where Egbert could pull the wheelbarrow over, sit on the guide rail fence, retrieve the quart from beneath the rug, and down a few hefty swallows. On hot days the quart was usually empty by the time he reached the store.

Groceries bought, Egbert started the long trip home. His second visit to the tavern was to enjoy another glass at the bar and purchase a quart to take with him in case he got thirsty along the road ahead.

The hot days of summer brought beads of sweat to Egbert's forehead and he made frequent stops as he climbed the first, long, steep hill. Sitting on the wheelbarrow, he mopped his brow with the blue bandanna he carried in his back pocket. As he rested, he reached under the rug for the bottle hidden there and cooled off with a long draught of refreshment. He sometimes didn't get past the first mile with anything left in the bottle. Then he had to go back to the tavern, still pushing the wheelbarrow and groceries, for another quart or two. This resupply generally saw him home on even the hottest days. It took time for Egbert to make his round trip to the store, but he was in no hurry—the passing hours meant nothing with a supply of beer close at hand.

SPEAKING OF THE HOURS OF THE DAY, the story goes that neither Willie B. nor his brother over in East Windham could tell time. Nevertheless, Willie took a fancy to a fine pocket watch displayed in the window of the emporium down in Windham. By scrimping and saving his money, he finally had enough to buy the watch. He carried it wherever he went, proudly showing it to everyone he met. He religiously wound the watch every evening and enjoyed listening to its measured beat and watching the hands make their turns around the ornately numbered face.

The brothers worked at odd jobs around the settlement and, as the afternoon dragged on one day, Willie asked, "Wonder what time it is?"

"Where's your watch?" his brother responded.

Willie pulled it from his pocket and snapped open the cover so both could see. "There she be," he said.

"Darned if she ain't," agreed his brother.

Willie closed the watch and replaced it in his pocket. They worked on until their stomachs grumbled and reminded them of supper. They didn't need the watch to tell what time it was after all.

A SPRING DAY, 1969

SPRING comes slowly to the Catskills. It's not that it doesn't want to get here; it's more that winter won't let go. Most everyone wishes this seasonal change could be rushed along but none more than those who are confined in an office far from the hills and wonder what it would be like to feel the warmness of the sun and the first gentle breezes of spring. In the days of the frontier I suppose this restlessness was called cabin fever but today the diagnosis is more likely spring fever. When boys and men exhibit the symptoms, the affliction is said to be fishing fever. It makes no difference whether the fish are biting or not, the urge is still there. Whatever the name, there is nothing to do but admit the disability and seek recovery. This is about a day when I was stricken and took to the woods.

It was seven miles from my home in West Kill, in the center of the Catskill Mountains, to the head of Spruceton Valley. Here the Devil's Path begins and winds through New York State's Forest Preserve, over five mountains, covering a distance of about twenty miles to its easterly terminus at Platte Clove. The first mountain crossed by the trail is Hunter Mountain. On the northerly side of this second highest peak in the Catskills is a privately-owned subsidiary mountain, the Colonel's Chair. This peak is the home of Hunter Mountain Ski Bowl, the mecca of winter sports enthusiasts. An addition was being made to the ski area and, when viewed from the highway, it appeared the upper reaches of the clearings for a new lift line were perilously close to the line of the state-owned lands. Although it was not part of my job description, I decided I was just the one to go on the ground to make sure the state land wasn't being compromised.

There had been a frost during the night. My lawn was a glistening white when I awoke and the thermometer stood at 28°. The early sun, already warming the top of the mountain in back of the house, promised a good day and a cloudless sky agreed.

It was eight o'clock when I pulled into the parking area at the beginning of the trail. The fields along the road had turned a brilliant green but the trees at the head of the valley had only just begun to bud and it would be another week or two before spring started its annual walk up the mountain. I shivered in the morning cold as I put on my pack, which contained only my lunch and some maps with which to locate myself when I reached the state land boundary.

The first part of the trail is relatively level and it was not long before I covered this at a swift pace to the accompaniment of a poor attempt to whistle my way along. The frost brought out the smell of the woods and the clearness of the air acted as a tonic. The rushing stream beside the trail ran high; a chipmunk chattered at my trespass in his domain; some birds inquired what my business was. The trail steepened and I slowed noticeably.

Soon I reached the point where an old lot line crossed. I had planned to leave the trail here and follow this and other lot lines to where the clearings were being made. When I compared the even grade of the trail with that of the old line, I wondered at the merit of my plan but decided to stick to it. The muscles of my legs protested at the steep slope and I realized the stagnation of winter was going to cause problems throughout the day. A deer left its bed at my approach and ran swiftly and bleating into the deeper woods. I suspected a fawn left behind and searched cautiously, but found nothing. As I rested leaning against an ancient yellow birch, two woodpeckers argued about me and, after apparently deciding I was all right, went about their job of finding breakfast. The loser of the argument, still having doubts, flew over to the birch, perched in the topmost branches, and quizzically cocked his head at me. Evidently he still didn't care for my looks because, after a few exploratory taps at the birch, he said as much to his companion and flew off.

The line was well marked and easily followed. After a time I left the birch and beech and entered the stand of spruce that ringed the top of the mountain. Some of these trees were over two feet through at the stump and their stately appearance called to mind Longfellow's "Druids of old." On a massive birch, an intruder in this spot, a large conk grew gleaming white in the sun. I overcame a desire to scratch my name on it and left it as it was. Just below the crest of the mountain I found a pile of stones built many years ago to mark a property corner. Beyond the corner the tree blazes became sparse, but I was able to follow the line with my compass. As I approached the height of land, the large trees gave way to the tangled and stunted growth that characterizes the tops of mountains of the Catskills. The witch hopple, dwarf spruce, scraggly beech, and interminable blackberry bushes made for difficult going. Through a break in the trees I saw the long scar made by the clearing operation and the stillness was shattered by the whine of a chain saw. I was back in the land of man.

From my point of observation I could see no work was going on between Rusk Mountain, where I was, and the ridge connecting Hunter Mountain with Colonel's Chair. There seemed no point in continuing to follow the lot line to the next pile of stones which was some distance down the northerly slope of the mountain. I turned to the right, hoping to pick up the northerly line of the state property before reaching the trail running through the saddle between Rusk and Hunter Mountains. I lost my hard-won elevation rapidly, but was compensated by the blanket of flowers that covered the ground. I have always envied those who can call these markers of spring by name. The fact that I cannot doesn't detract from their beauty and courage in following so close behind the retreating snows of winter. However, I did recognize a trillium growing off by itself near a downed birch; it waved in the gentle breeze to return my nod of greeting.

As the trail became visible through the trees, I intersected the state-land boundary line. I looked across the hollow to the next ridge and saw that the cutting seemed to be entirely on the ski area side of the line. The relative ease of the trail when contrasted with a further loss of elevation and the following steep climb up the ridge, prompted me to greater effort; however, the inactivity of winter was taking its toll. A bubbling spring offered a welcome drink and an excuse to rest. The chain saw stopped and the sounds of the woods took over. Another woodpecker was drilling out the top of a birch and a squirrel scolded from his perch in a nearby maple.

It was a short walk up to the saddle where the trail turned left to follow the height of land. I had hiked this trail many times over the years and remembered each climb with pleasure. I passed the John Robb Lean-to and soon reached the junction with the trail leading to Colonel's Chair. I turned left down it. About a quarter of a mile along I crossed the state boundary line and was immediately confronted by the opening made by the clearing operation. It stopped just short of the line at the edge of the trail and stretched straight down to the stream at the foot of the ridge. It was quiet. The stumps of the cut trees stood mute telling of man's seemingly uncontrollable urge to turn every piece of land into some kind of production. The sap seeping from the stumps was still frozen but was beginning to melt. Although it was time for lunch and a flat rock offered an ideal table, this didn't seem the place for it. Back at the trail junction, another flat rock with a balsam tree beside it to lean against made a perfect seat for my lunch of a cheese sandwich and thermos of milk.

My mission was accomplished; the Forest Preserve was untouched and I had the afternoon to roam the mountain. I decid-

ed to continue on up the trail and visit my village neighbor, Joe D.,
who was the observer stationed at the Hunter Mountain fire tower
or observation station as it's officially called. The trail leveled and
it didn't take long to cover the mile to the tower. Patches of snow
dotted the thick forest floor and, just before the last short climb to
the tower, I waded through a lengthy stretch of it still over one foot
deep.

Joe saw me coming and waved a greeting from the cabin atop
the tower. I took off my pack and climbed the stairs, pausing at
each landing to take in the expanding view. My first visit to the
tower was in 1944 when I camped overnight at the site. I still
looked forward to every trip to this place and today's visit was no
exception. As I climbed, the entire Catskills unfolded on a 360°
sweep and I recognized many distant peaks I had climbed in years
past. The works of man dotted the valleys but paled into insignificance as the mountains overshadowed them.

Joe was glad to see me as I was his first visitor of the day. We
talked about the condition of the trail, the upcoming forest fire season, a bear hunt he had been on last fall, the porcupine problem,
the variety of visitors to the tower, and generally solved a few of
the troubles of the world. With the aid of his field glasses, I picked
out many landmarks and watched a hawk circle over a nearby
ridge before disappearing behind it in a swift, graceful dive. It was
a relaxing hour and I left with the feeling that this man, this tower,
this trail, and others like them were not out of place in the Forest
Preserve but, instead, enhanced this vast public ownership.

As I reached the woods on the downhill trail, I turned to wave
a farewell to Joe and received an answering wave in reply. My
return trip was easier with fewer stops for rest. Just past the John
Robb Lean-to, I took the short side trail to the spring for a cold
drink of the clear water flowing from between the rocks. I paused
at each lookout along the way and marveled at the vistas smiling
back at me. News of my coming was sent ahead by the denizens of
the mountains and the woods were quiet as I approached, an
unwanted trespasser in their world. When I reached my car, I
paused before starting home to savor a last few minutes of my out-

door day but finally, and somewhat unwillingly, re-entered the busy world.

In years to come, my recollection of this day would be pleasant. I was tired and my muscles ached, but both feelings were overcome by the experiences my senses had enjoyed. I had heard and talked to the dwellers of the forest; I had smelled the pure smells of the woods awakening from a frosty night; I had seen the mountains as they once were and viewed the magnificent distance of the Catskills from one of their highest peaks; I had felt the warm sun and the sensation of freedom of the hills; I had savored the taste of a squashed cheese sandwich flavored with the scent of balsam and had drunk from the coolness of a mountain spring. Perhaps most important, I had been witness, on this spring day, to the birth of a season.

A SUMMER DAY, 1998

I COULDN'T HAVE PICKED A BETTER DAY. It had rained most of the night and the morning sky held ominous grey clouds here and there suggesting the rain might turn about to come again. However, a patch of blue in the west gave promise and I decided to trust in it. It was a spur-of-the-moment thing but it sure felt like a good day to hike to the fire tower on Hunter Mountain by the Spruceton Trail and see what was going on up there.

I had first visited the tower in the early 1940s when it was sited about a thousand feet southeasterly along the summit ridge from the actual peak of the mountain where it was now located. Then I had camped overnight at the top of a ledge on the Spruceton side and had returned many times over the years but not lately. The tower was abandoned now, although efforts were afoot to restore it. I wondered how it had survived the last few years of neglect.

I expected changes in the valley, but not nearly as many as confronted me as I drove along. Houses I remembered were no longer there or had been remodeled beyond my recognition. Others stood in meadows where cows used to pasture and the names on most of the mail boxes were unfamiliar. However, mountains I knew reared up on both sides of the road and circled the end of the valley. I could make out the tower far away on the imposing ridge that faced me.

I pulled into the parking area just off the main road which, at the upper end, was a narrow two lanes, paved with dirt. Even the parking lot had changed. It had previously been farther along at the end of a single-tracked lane traced by stone walls along each side. Even though it was a week day, I had expected to find another car or two in the lot but mine was the first of the morning and, as I was to discover when I returned in the afternoon, the only car then as well. I never did encounter anyone and evidently had the mountain to myself for the day.

I heaved my knapsack onto my back. Not much was in it, but it felt heavier than when I had packed it early that morning with a ham sandwich, two jugs of lemonade, a jacket, two cameras, and a few odds and ends I probably wouldn't need. I picked up my hiking staff, something I had scoffed at in my youth but now accepted as a concession to passing years.

The trail led from the parking lot into the lane. In the 1800s, this had been the main route from Spruceton to the Schoharie below Hunter and the trail followed it to the saddle between Rusk and Hunter Mountains. It climbed only slightly past the old parking lot now grown over with trees and brush. Hunter Brook babbled along on the left.

About half a mile on, the trail turned sharply to the left and crossed the brook on a wooden bridge. Straight ahead of the turn and 100 feet or so beyond it, the Spruceton Lean-to had once been located. In those days, it and others like it were called open camps. All traces of it were gone, the small clearing was empty with saplings gradually filling it in.

Beyond the bridge the way steepened, but the old road offered a steady grade and a pleasant perspective. I paused often for short rests, far more than in olden times when I usually took the mountain from bottom to top without a break. Giving reason to some of these stops, I marveled at the workmanship of the original stone-box culverts—and there were many—that drained storm water under the road. Over a century later, they still did the job they had been built to do.

I finally reached the saddle between the mountains where the old road dropped down Taylor Hollow heading for the Schoharie. The trail turned right and weaved its way along the ridge of Hunter Mountain. It became much steeper; the regular, gentle grade had been left behind. It climbed right, then left, then back again, zig-zagging over outcroppings of ledge rock. Loose stones rolled underfoot. I rested more often and suspected the trail had been relocated; it surely hadn't been this rugged years ago.

In time, I passed the short branch trail leading to a spring on the right. Not far past that, I came to the John Robb Lean-to. I stopped for a longer break, climbing onto the large rock on the opposite side of the trail to admire the sweeping vista of Spruceton Valley framed by the bulk of Rusk and Evergreen Mountains on one side and West Kill Mountain and North Dome on the other.

I went on and soon came to a sign noting the elevation was 3500 feet with camping prohibited above it. This left another 500 feet to surmount before reaching the summit of Hunter at 4040 feet. Mercifully the trail leveled out a short distance beyond the junction with the trail running northerly to Colonel's Chair. Along this stretch, just around a slight bend in the trail, I caught the first sight of the tower, still a long way ahead and much farther than I remembered it to be. Had it been moved back down the ridge, I wondered, or was the distance perceived by younger eyes shorter than that of later years?

Beyond the level run, the trail climbed again. I recognized it as the last slope before the summit and hurried on. It turned left into a large clearing covered with a scattering of stones and filling in with knee-high spruce trees. The observer's cabin was boarded up, home only to the porcupines that occasionally took lunch from the boards of the front porch.

The tower loomed over it; nine flights of stairs climbed to the cab at the top. The roof of this was gone as were the windows that had once closed its four sides. It looked sad and forlorn, its moment of glory in the past. Even though signs warned the tower was closed to the public, I decided to climb it anyway. The structure seemed solid throughout and the steps of the stairs were firmly bolted in place.

At about the third landing, I topped the trees surrounding the clearing. The wind picked up and blew stronger as I went higher. The grey clouds were gone, now replaced by high, fleecy, white ones that scudded across a bright blue sky. The air was clear, vistas spread out in whatever direction I looked. Small clearings sprinkled the landscapes all around; faraway roads drew pencil lines through the deep valleys; villages and settlements clustered here and there.

All this, however, paled into insignificance when I reached the top. The surrounding world seemed to have no horizon. The deep green of the summer mountains stretched beyond reality; range after range rolled on forever into a magnificent distance. One could—once in a while, anyway—go home again; these sights were as I remembered them. God might, indeed, be in His heaven, but surely He had passed this way in the beginning and laid down these old hills as He went.

I was reminded of the words Natty Bumppo, the Leather-Stocking, had used when describing what he saw as he looked out from a high ledge on the escarpment of the Catskills.

"What see you when you get there?" he was asked.

"Creation!" replied Natty, "all creation, lad."

A MINK HOLLOW SPRING

IN THE YEARS OF MY YOUTH, the winter woods called. I loved waking on mornings when the mountains were cloaked in white. I hoped then the roads were so deep with snow the school bus couldn't make its daily run. When that happened (which was rarely), the day was mine. Well, not really the whole day, only that part after the cows were milked, the young stock fed, the horses watered and their mangers filled with hay, the paths and driveway shoveled, and whatever else those in charge at my house thought of to keep me busy. Then I could strap on my skis and head for the back sap bush to wend my way in the solitary woods and leave my marks in the untracked snow.

This affinity with cold and winter and snow didn't wane even when I became lost in the mountains for the only time in my life. It happened when my father sent my uncle and I to the sap bush after a late winter storm to rehang buckets blown down by violent gusts of wind. Our task finished, we headed into a blinding snow-fall following a roundabout track back to the barn. Confident in my sense of direction, I predicted that if we climbed the ridge ahead, we would drop into The Notch above West Kill not far from our farm. As we descended, the snow stopped and the sky cleared to a brilliant blue. I recognized nothing in the valley below. I had no idea where we were. We stopped to enquire at the first farm-house we reached. We were in Halcott, the farmer said and won-dered from where we had come. It wasn't till then I realized that instead of climbing the ridge we had actually gone up and over the whole range and into the next town.

I now know this allure of winter was a symptom of growing up. I was seeking challenge as all boys do—and girls, too, I sup-pose. But that's behind me. With advancing years, spring and the reawakening of the countryside has become a more-meaningful time of the year.

To be part of it and to satisfy my curiosity about a boundary line, I traveled up the Spruceton Valley one fine day. Spring had arrived down along the Hudson where we then lived. The crocus-es and daffodils were in bloom, shadbush was beginning to blos-som, songbirds sang long before my alarm clock rang in the morn-ings. Spring comes too fast in the lowlands; I wanted to experience its more-deliberate pace in the mountains of home.

Signs of it were well-hidden as I drove through The Notch and made the turn at the bottom of the hill. Only two or three fisher-man's cars were parked off the road beside the West Kill. The floods of a few weeks before had ravaged the stream. Deep pools that had once harbored the wary trout had been scoured and trans-formed.

I parked at the foot of Mink Hollow, shouldered my light pack, and started up the mountain. As I climbed, it grew quiet. The wild, plunging stream was silent. Why, I wondered? A loud noise and then another, like a board hitting a flat surface sounded up ahead. The hollow leveled and opened wide before me. Well-chewed stumps of poplar, soft maple, and even hemlock dotted the shore of an expanse of open water and the wet, spongy ground surrounding it. Beavers were at work here, rebuilding dams washed away by the recent floods. Sap dripped down the side of the pointed stumps. Two ducks startled me as they beat their way across the pond and disappeared over the ridge. Instinct told them spring was coming to the North Country and directed them along the flyway blazed by earlier generations of their kind.

Songbirds chirped at my passing to ask why I was there. I didn't know who they were—my knowledge of bird lore doesn't extend much beyond being able to identify crows, blue jays, and a cardinal now and then. That, however, doesn't mute the notes of those who sing a welcome to spring.

The buds of the trees and shrubs were swelled almost to the bursting point. The color within that would soon cover the landscape was still hidden. Was I too early to see spring begin? As if in reply, I saw skunk cabbage sprouting green out of the muck in wet spots along the stream. Then I noticed a jack-in-the-pulpit swaying on its stem, the purple color of its blossom just beginning to appear.

I climbed slowly. A sign of advancing years? Certainly not, I deluded myself, arguing that my moderate pace was so I could have more time to contemplate and enjoy the surroundings. After a number of pauses to rest, I continued on, my goal the notch between West Kill Mountain and North Dome and the boundary line that crossed there. Patches of snow covered the ground on the north side of the larger rocks and sheets of thick ice hung from ledges on my right. I was too early; I would have to come back another time if I wanted to see spring in the making. Well, maybe not.

As I topped the ridge on the shoulder of North Dome and

looked down to the half-acre pond nestling in the saddle between the two mountains, I noticed shoots of green reaching through the scattered snow cover in the open area around the shallow pond. I knew what they were. The much-maligned leek may not measure up to the image of bold, showy colors we expect of the season, but old-timers consider its onion-like taste and scent a spring tonic. It sometimes served another purpose. Boys looking for a way to skip school have been known to eat a mess of leeks just before the school bus arrived. The pungent smell remaining on the breath of those who ate them was reason enough for the driver to deny them entry into the bus. If they did make it to school, chances are the teacher might not allow them into the classroom.

I had come prepared, expecting to find this fresh, tender plant somewhere on the mountain. I pulled a few. Their sharp smell filled the air. I breathed deeply; it was a tonic indeed. I spread them thickly on my cheese sandwich. I might not be allowed in the house when I returned home, but spring comes just once a year and I didn't want to pass up the chance to taste it.

I also felt spring as I sat on a flat, cold rock next to the pond— real early spring in fact. The sky had turned gray as I climbed the hollow. Mist settled around me. Wind whistled through the notch, swirling the mist about and spraying me with fine droplets. It was cold and warm at the same time, as if winter didn't want to let go and spring was trying to push it aside. Eating a cheese sandwich garnished with a wild, savory plant while sitting between two seasons is an experience one remembers.

It ended too soon. The storm announced by the dark clouds didn't materialize where I was, but I heard thunder rumbling far away in a direction I couldn't quite figure out. A sound of spring? Surely it was.

I walked a different route down the mountain, staying close to the stream draining its slopes. Birds sang their songs for me; the rattle of a woodpecker echoed across the hollow; a chipmunk scolded from his stance on a log beside the old road I was following. I stopped by the beaver pond. It was quiet; the beaver were out of sight somewhere, probably watching as I stood there. Then, almost as if it knew what I was listening for, a lone peeper on the far side of the water began his paean to the new season.

I heard another sound; a honking came out of the mist. Then the characteristic V of a skein of geese appeared and began to dip low as if to settle on the beaver pond. Seeing me, their leader thought better of it and called his followers back onto their northern path. As the saying goes, one robin does not make a spring, but this string of geese winging its way toward distant Canada was surely towing it along behind.

I reached my car tired in limb, but fresh in mind. I had seen spring, heard it, smelled it, tasted it, and felt it. Life was being reborn in the mountains; all was right with the world. The boundary line? I had forgotten all about it as I basked in the wonder of the hills. Ah, well, I thought, I would just have to go back another time. Maybe next spring.

ON THE TRANSIT LINE

THE FIRST TIME I set up a transit was in October of 1953. I was enrolled as a forestry major at the University of Maine at Orono but had signed up for a number of courses with the engineers. This one was indexed in the catalog as Ce3, Field Work and Plotting. We were a crew of three—Ed Salmon, Dave Trask, and I thrown together by the fact we had come in near the tail end of the alpha bet race.

We spent most of that semester on what was called the Beta Traverse, a six-sided figure that took us around three fraternity houses and the infirmary. We ran the traverse and a number of level loops, tied in everything that didn't move, and drafted a map that delineated it all including contour lines and the species and location of every tree scattered around the site.

I don't recall the make and model of the transit but suspect it may have been a Gurley Light Mountain or maybe a K&E. It read to the nearest minute with estimates to 30". We turned every angle twice and took the mean of the two. The transit may have been accurate but evidently I wasn't too sharp operating it. Our closure for the six angles was out 2' 15". Possibly Ed or Dave, while holding backsights and foresights were distracted by a passing co-ed at a critical moment.

To use the term loosely, that was my first survey. In the intervening fifty years I have been involved in a few more. The seven personal narratives included in this section relate the experiences that made some of them more memorable than others.

THE 500-FOOT TAPE

I AM CONTINUALLY AMAZED by the array of electronic wiz-ardry pictured in the pages of the surveying magazine that comes along every month or so. Other advertisements offer instruments and equipment of the type I'm still using and describe them as antiques. That tells me I come from a different age. An article in a recent issue was more than a little humbling.

It described a "sports competition" held at a recent convention of land surveyors and, in particular, an event called "throwing the chain." According to the account, not many participants succeed-ed in accomplishing the feat, yet I do it almost every day I'm in the field. For those not familiar with the term, it's the method by which a flat, steel, measuring tape 1 chain, 100 feet, 200 feet, or whatever length can be done up into a single coil. The tape is first drawn hand over hand in equal lengths and laid into the palm of the left hand (assuming the one attempting the process is right handed, that is) resulting in a number of hanging and concentric figure-eight loops. By grasping the layers of tape on top of the cross of the figure eight in one hand and the bottom layers in the other, the sur-veyor can, by a deft twist of both wrists, "throw" the tape into a single loop. If the tape is dropped at any point in the process, a God-awful snarl ensues and no amount of cursing will untangle it.

The author of the article stated he had never seen anyone throw a tape as long as 300 feet. Well, here's the story of the 500-foot tape.

Ed was continually on the lookout for new ways to increase the efficiency and output of his state survey crew. When a 500-foot tape first appeared in a catalog, he decided we should have one. With a tape of that length we could set up longer shots and get more accurate measurements by stretching the tape from station to station and reading vertical angles from one to the next, or so went Ed's reasoning. The catalog didn't list a reel for the tape; no matter, it was ordered anyway.

When it finally came, it lay coiled like a giant mainspring with-in a deep-sided shipping box and we knew it was trouble. Stretching it out full length without any kinks took some doing, but we somehow accomplished it with a minimum of foul language. We were then faced with the question of what to do with it. With no reel, the only answer was to throw it. I did it up in 8-foot lengths and had more than a handful of loops (sixty-two in fact) when I reached the end. When I tried to throw it, that practiced twist of the wrists that worked so well with 1-, 2-, and 3-chain tapes turned into a struggle. It was kind of like having a tiger by the tail and it nearly threw me. We all (except Ed, that is, who left the menial tasks to us) became adept at throwing the monster, but only after many unsuccessful attempts.

Using the tape was just as challenging. Unthrowing it wasn't any easier than the other way around. Laying it out ready for the day's work required a long walk to weave it around trees and over rocks and runs of water up whatever remote Catskill peak we were confronting that day. (Every survey in the Catskills is up; no one I know remembers any that went down.) Stretching the tape from the tack on the lower station to the head of the transit on the upper one required a major effort. I don't recall the tape's specifications for tension and sag, but I'm sure we never matched them. One rainy day while we were in the office Dan, the assistant on the crew, tried to figure the pounds of pull necessary to take out sag in the tape and came up with something exceeding 40 tons. After deriving that absurd (maybe it wasn't) figure, he gave up.

In the winter, we were careful to tie the leather thong on the front end of the tape to something solid. We learned the necessity for that after once watching it slide easily over the snow down half a mountain to end up piled in a jumble at the foot of a ledge. Finding an end somewhere in the mess, threading it through coil after coil of tangle, and walking off each length took most of the morning.

It presented other hazards as well. One survey ran a great lot line up a ridge of Balsam Mountain, climbing 1600 feet in elevation over a distance of about 1-1/2 miles where we tied into a previous survey to get a closure. Our later computations disclosed we had dropped 100 feet somewhere. Ed was sure it was in that line going up the ridge and sent two of us out on a cold, winter's day to check measure each shot in the traverse. We did, but didn't locate the error.

Instead of throwing the tape at the top of the mountain, I decided to wait until we reached the flat land at the bottom. I put my partner on the upper end of the tape and took the front end, starting swiftly down anxious to get back to a warm car. The ridge had evolved over millennia into a series of shelves marked by ledges 6 feet or so high. As it turned out, when I reached a gentle slope and increased my pace, my partner was at one of the ledges. We were so far apart his entreaties for me to slow down were lost in the distance. Knowing the consequence if he let go of the tape, he hung on and took some ledges at a jump and others by sliding over them on his back. At the foot of the mountain I asked why he was covered with snow and had such a wild look in his eye. His response is better not written here.

A later catalog included a reel for the 500-foot tape and, at our urging, Ed ordered it. It was an ungainly wooden contraption consisting of three collapsible spokes topped by U-shaped extensions to hold the tape, a fold-out handle to turn the reel, and a single pin to keep everything in place once all the movable parts were aligned. It worked all right for a while, but the inevitable happened. One fine summer day on top of a mountain (as usual), as the last few feet of the tape were being wound on the reel, the pin fell out, the reel collapsed, and all 500 feet dropped into a heap on the ground. We laboriously straightened it out, walking out each length as we threaded it through the tangled skein. It was late in the day and we rushed the job. Unnoticed kinks developed as we laid the tape through and around the trees. As I was pulling it into figure eights, I came to an end at less than 100 feet. We then discovered the kinks, all of which had snapped. The piece I was holding turned out to be the longest. We left the pieces as they were and they lay there yet rusting, one hopes, into well-deserved oblivion. The reel ended up in Ed's fireplace. We went back to our old 3-chain and 200-foot tapes and never again spoke of the 500-foot tape—whenever Ed was around, that is.

THE WINTER WOODS

IT CERTAINLY IS CURIOUS why this driveway is so much longer in winter than it is the rest of the year. The snow gets deeper and heavier the longer I shovel. Of course, if I waited until it stopped snowing, it wouldn't pile up behind me. But I can't wait for that; a full day stretches out ahead and it's time to be on my way. As my grandmother would have said, "Don't shilly-shally around."

I finally reach the street. Only an inch or two covers the driveway back by the garage. The snow continues—big, fluffy flakes come down, swirling and whirling in the breeze. That wind could build some troublesome drifts if it keeps up. A good job done, I say to myself as I hang the snow shovel on the nail just inside the garage door; however, maybe it's not done. Sure enough, here comes the snowplow. I know that guy parks behind the house on the corner and waits till I have the driveway cleared. Then he revs up, drops the plow, and bears down in my direction with a big grin on his face as he picks up speed. Snow flies and builds up in front of the blade as he comes around the circle. As usual, he leaves most of it for me and half buries the mailbox in the bargain. Cursing just a bit, I take down the shovel and confront the heap of snow now blocking my way into the street.

When I finally get that out of the way, I holler in at the kitchen door. "At last, I'm off to the mountains. I'll be back sometime this afternoon."

"Just remember, you're not as young as you once were," Dot cautions.

"Huh," I snort—to myself, of course. "Age has nothing to do with it. Still would take two men and a boy to keep up." I know that's not true and she does too, but it sounds good.

"Once" was thirty-five years earlier when I surveyed that farm over in Dry Brook. It's now being sold by the couple who bought it back then and their lawyer advised them to have the boundary lines inspected by a surveyor. Bet they were surprised to find me in the 'phone book and were probably more surprised I was still fit enough to walk those lines, especially with over a foot of snow on the ground.

When I took up the surveyors' trade, I imagined spending my days in the field, off the beaten path, looking for lost corners and boundary lines in deep woods and over high mountains. Little did I suspect I'd end up in an office and be frustrated by inept bureaucrats and politicians who assured taxpayers their hard-earned money was being spent wisely and efficiently when all the time they knew it wasn't. Once those years passed, I headed again for the field, trying to put distance between myself and the insistent jangling of the telephone that had then plagued my life.

The drivers of the plows over in Dry Brook must get the same training as the one on our street. Snow is heaped high on both sides of the road in front of the old farm. Even though the owners don't live here anymore, the snowplow driver could have scooped out a place to pull over in the access road leading into the property. He didn't. I park as close to the snowbank as I can get, expecting the car to be blocked in when I return later in the day. Chances are, the plow and driver are hiding up around the corner, watching and waiting until I disappear down the hill.

The downhill walk to the stream is easy going. The snow is light and loose; snowshoes wouldn't help. Just as well, I had forgotten to throw them in when I loaded up in the early morning.

The stream is frozen over. The temperature has regularly been well below freezing for the last two or three weeks. The thermometer on my pack registers 10°. The water gurgles as it seeks a channel under the ice.

I leave the roadway and strike off through the woods looking for the northerly boundary line. The limbs of the hemlocks droop low under their burden of snow. I hit a few with my ax, but that dislodges the snow on the upper limbs which drops on my head and shoulders and down the neck of my jacket. However, this is part of the surveyors' lot. We seldom travel trails and roads. Our way runs over other terrain—up craggy ledges and into murky swamps, over steep hills and down rolling ridges, past tumbling waterfalls and through placid waters, into open forest and caught in the tangle of briars and brambles. It's the variety of nature and discoveries waiting along the transit line that take us off the well-traveled paths used by others.

I finally find the line. The blazes I put on the trees long ago have grown over and catch only a surveyor's practiced eye. I follow them down the hill to the stream bank. I hit the ice a few times with my ax. It sounds solid, but cracks ominously as I cross over. The line on the far side follows an old stone wall. It's hidden by the snow, its track up the hill resembles the mound (on a grander scale, of course) left by the mole which lives under the sod in our back yard.

The hill is a lot steeper than I remember and I stop often to rest. I pretend it's the deep snow that slows me down. The view off to the west widens as I climb. When I finally reach the back corner, the noon whistle sounds off in the distance. I brush the snow from a flat rock and sit leaning against the maple tree behind it. The snow has stopped. The sky has cleared and the sun warms my face. From my perch on top of the ridge, it seems I look out to forever. The old surveyor I first worked with said the Catskills were "The land of the magnificent distance." Indeed, they are. Their peaks and valleys chase each other on and on as far as I can see. The snow covers the land like frosting on a cake and looks just as inviting. It's rewards like the scenes around me that make the morning toil worthwhile. I linger long. My lemonade—turned to slush by the cold—and peanut butter and jam sandwich become a gourmet meal because of the beauty of my surroundings.

The rest of the day is anticlimactic; I easily locate the remaining boundary lines and corners. It's all downhill from there, except for the short climb to the road on the other side of the stream. The snowplow has been by; the side of my car is plastered over with hard-packed snow. The driver's chuckle of satisfaction seems to hang in the air beside it. I imagine the driveway will be plowed shut when I get home. It is.

However, even that doesn't dim the pleasure I found in the winter woods. It's a treat to behold close-up the charms of any season, but the experience becomes truly magical in the quiet of winter.

SHOOTING POLARIS

THE MIRACLES OF MODERN ELECTRONICS can be more than
a little bewildering to vintage surveyors who remember how to
use a slide rule and can still decipher traverse tables and logarithms. Yesterday's transits could turn angles accurate to a minute
with estimates to 30". Over time, technology developed theodo-
lites accurate to 10" and, then, to a single second. "On-board" computers now provide digital read-outs to a tenth of a second. Distances along the traverse used to be measured by chainmen who
sighted along a hand level, dangled plumb bobs over ledges, and
waded swift-flowing and ice-cold streams trying to keep the tape
out of the water. That antiquated way of doing things has also
yielded to electronics—distances today are determined with
uncanny accuracy to a thousandth of a foot.

All that sounds impressive and it is, of course, but is it really
necessary to know the length and breadth of a parcel of land to
that degree of exactness? It may be when dealing with a lot in the
middle of some sprawling city but certainly not on the steep side
hills of the Catskill Mountains. As my old mentor used to say,
"What's 10 feet in the woods?" The answer for the owner of a 160-
acre lot up at the dead end of some deep hollow is "Not much."

While cleaning out some old files in a recent fit of energy, I
came across a stack of the forms we once used to compute bearings
from observations on Polaris. They were filled with many long-for-
gotten terms such as local hour angle, Greenwich civil time, polar
distance, true altitude, log sine and cosine, etc. What with satellites
and global positioning systems, I suppose surveyors no longer
"shoot" the North Star to convert magnetic bearings over to true
and that's too bad. Some of the best (and worst) meals I remember
were while sitting around an open fire deep in the woods waiting
for the stars (or the one star we were looking for, that is) to come
out.

One that ranks right up near the top of the list, and in the now-
it-can-be-told category, was over on the Beaverkill. We had run a
spur line from the state lands on the mountain down to a small

clearing near the headwaters of a stream which fairly boiled with trout fingerlings 3 and 4 inches in length. This was sacred ground (or, at least, sacred water) that belonged to an exclusive, ultra-private, fishing club steeped in tradition. Theodore Gordon, John Burroughs, and others of hallowed name had fished here. For all we knew, Izaak Walton himself may have cast a line or two in this legendary stream.

No matter how it sounds, we weren't trespassing. The road running deep in the interior of the club property provided a near access to the state lands. We still had a steep hike of a mile or so from the end of the road to where we wanted to be, but it was a lot better than climbing up and over the mountain range from the other side. Ed, the chief of our survey crew, was well-known and respected by the club members and its caretaker, an irascible mountain man who brooked no excuse from those unlucky souls he happened to discover on the club's side of its well-posted boundary line.

He had trusted Ed with a key to the gate and permission to drive to the end of the club's road where we could leave our car for the day and walk the remaining distance across the club property to the state land beyond. Not surprisingly, this special dispensation from on high came with a caveat—"No fishing and, in fact, stay away from the stream except where you have to cross it." Ed appreciated the sanctity of these waters and assured the club officers—and especially the caretaker—we were there to do our job and nothing would stay us from that charge no matter how tempted we might be.

We planned ahead to observe the polestar on a day we knew Ed had to be in Albany. We had seen too many of those small trout day after day to just ignore them. After all, we reasoned, the club owned miles and miles of the Beaverkill and had more fish than they knew what to do with. If a few went the way of a fish fry to feed hungry and deserving surveyors, well, they'd still have plenty left over.

We came well-prepared that day. Each of us had been assigned a part of the evening meal. One brought a hefty tin of freshly-baked brownies (not by him, of course); another had butter, salt, pepper, and bags of potato chips; a third had bottles of soft drinks that we set to cool in the water of the stream; and the last brought a large, iron skillet. After adding the transit, tripod, flashlights, axes, chain, other surveying paraphernalia, and our lunches, we could have used a pack mule.

We did run a bit of transit line even though it came down a steady drizzle most of the day. We persisted, hoping for a clearing before supper. By late afternoon, blue sky took over and we hiked down to the clearing. We lugged stones out from the woods and built a fireplace, collected dry wood and last, but by no means least, dipped a goodly number of wriggling trout from the water. This far upstream, the fish weren't big enough to catch with a line and hook, but they seemed ready to jump into the small net we had brought along. That little, they didn't have to be cleaned. Popped into a frying pan swimming with hot, snapping, crackling butter and lightly seasoned, they curled into crispy morsels that tasted uncommonly good.

It was a banquet, no other word quite fits. It was such a grand experience, we almost forgot why we were there. As the fire died down and after eating as much as we could hold, we got to it. The star was right where it was supposed to be and we turned a number of precisely timed angles to it. We doused the fire, packed up, and hiked, lighting our way by flashlight, back to the car.

A couple of weeks later, the caretaker approached Ed saying he had found the remains of a campfire and evidence of a fish fry on up the stream beyond where we usually left the car. He wondered if we had seen any unauthorized people on the club's property. Well, heck no, we told Ed, vowing to be on special alert for any such sinners from then on. I don't think Ed ever bought that story, but he questioned us no further. Maybe he too had enjoyed a stream-side fish fry or two in days gone by.

THE ANCIENT LANDMARK

MOST FOLKS have at least a passing knowledge of natural selection, survival of the fittest, and all that other Darwinian stuff and also understand about creatures and plants having natural enemies that keep things in balance. It's not so commonly known that land surveyors have enemies, natural and otherwise. No, not the landowner who is sure the surveyor of the adjoining lot is taking some of his land. That's usually because the complainant hasn't bothered to get his own survey and bases his knowledge of the boundary lines on what the previous owner told him when he bought the place and who got his information from the owner before him and so on and so on. The surveyor's enemies are the bulldozer and chain saw or, more correctly, those who operate these internal (infernal?) combustion menaces.

The bulldozer driver fixes his eye on the flatland surveyor, generally an older member of the species who picks and chooses his surveys carefully and doesn't take on anything more strenuous than house-lot subdivisions, ball fields, tennis courts, and the like. As he goes merrily along setting precise lines of stakes this way and that, the bulldozer guy sits perched on his machine, motor idling, waiting for the surveyor and his crew to pack up for the day. He then shifts into gear, lowers his blade, and lays waste to every stake in sight.

The chain saw operator is the bane of the deep woods, mountain surveyor, that rugged individual who's young in heart and spirit and wouldn't know a piece of level ground if he saw one. I count myself in this latter category, mainly because I served my novitiate in the Catskills where every boundary line runs uphill. This surveyor can easily be picked out of a crowd. He walks kind of tilted over to one side because his off leg is shorter than the other from many years of walking sideways across steep slopes. The chain saw guy doesn't wait in ambush for his prey; he's out there months or years ahead cutting down line-marked trees and leaving tangled tops right where the surveyor needs to run his transit line.

I've dealt with both of these adversaries and others too unsavory to be mentioned or, at least, the results of their handiworks. Here are the stories.

THE CORNER I was looking for was described in an 1865 deed as "a stone standing on the southwesterly side of a spring." An earlier and well-respected surveyor had passed that way in January of 1940 and noted the corner in his fieldbook to be "a point on a slope of rock west of road." He came back that July and "set capped iron pipe in drill hole @ about 2' south of wire fence and about 7' North of base of fallen 16" Maple. Laid stones around pipe."

With all those directions, I anticipated a proverbial "walk in the park" when I set out to run the line that angled at the corner. It wasn't. The corner was gone or, to be more truthful, I couldn't find it. I tried running a line in from both directions but that didn't work. To begin with, I couldn't find the back corner of the line coming in from the north. And nothing in the descriptions said just where on the road the beginning point was on the southeast. The spring was there all right but it was actually a wide wet area fed by a seep at the foot of a ledge. The fallen maple had turned to duff long ago. And, as usual in the Shawangunks, sloping rocks were all over the place and not one had a drill hole with a capped pipe set on it, in it, or beside it.

A couple of weeks later, I went back for another try. The first time around I had noticed a few scattered stones that looked sort of suspicious beside one of those sloping rocks. Examining them more closely, I decided the stones hadn't grown that way. I moved them aside one by one until down in the dirt at the edge of the wet area, I uncovered a corroded 6" length of pipe with a cap. The remainder had rusted away in the intervening fifty plus years. I hauled in some more stones from nearby, built a proper corner, and stuck the piece of pipe in the top.

A few years after that while driving by on the road, I heard the fearsome roar of a bulldozer off in the woods. Sure enough, there it was tearing up the landscape building a road where one didn't belong. That part already constructed had hit the corner dead on.

The stones and the capped piece of pipe were gone, probably now a part of the base of the road. The sloping rock had been blasted to smithereens and the seep was filled in. Such is progress.

THE NORTHWESTERLY CORNER of the Nineteen Partner Tract is—or, more correctly, was—a real antique treasure. The 1799 map of the tract said it was "A double black oak beging of 19 parter Tract." The description in the partition of the tract dated the same year called the corner "a double Black Oak Tree marked with three notches and a cross over them standing at the Edge of a hill."

On an earlier survey I had found the southwesterly corner of Lot 1 of the tract and noted the northwesterly line was marked, in part anyway, by a stone wall. The double oak was a corner in the line of Lot 8 some 76 chains (nearly a mile) away and the point of beginning of a survey I was to start work on.

To be sure I had the right tree—or the right point to begin from; after all, I didn't expect to find the tree after all those years—I decided to run a rough compass line out of the Lot 1 corner. The stone wall continued intermittently all along the tract line and I had no trouble following it as I chained lot after lot. When I neared the last few chains of the total distance, I was surprised to see a massive double oak tree up ahead. It stood at the brow of a hill and at the point of intersection of the stone wall I had been following with another running off to the southwest. I was thrilled at finding what I supposed was the original corner tree and started the traverse of my survey without taking time to look for the "three notches and a cross over them" that had first marked the tree those many years ago.

That oversight bothered me and I decided to visit the site again for the express purpose of looking for those original markings. As things turned out, it wasn't until four years later when I got back to the tree. I had waited too long; a logger on the adjoining lot had gotten there before me.

He had dropped one half of the double tree and hauled it off to the mill leaving a scarred stump as testimony to his wanton disregard of history. The cutting of one boll of the tree had removed part of the support of the other and it lay profaned on the ground. I looked it over carefully, even crawling beneath it to look at the underside, but didn't find the old marks. They must have been on the log taken away.

WHILE THE CALLOUS DISREGARD FOR CORNERS set in 1865 and 1799 is bad enough, neither equaled the antiquity of one set in 1749. That's the year Ebeneezer Wooster ran the east line of the Hardenburgh Patent.

Ebeneezer began at the stream which then ran out of North Lake into South Lake up in the northeast corner of the Catskills. His notes say "I began at the Cartrigeh Kill [now known as Kaaterskill Creek] where made a Monument of Stone Round a crocked Chestnut oak tree." He then ran southerly as called for in the 1708 grant of the Patent "by the Bounds of Kingstown Hurley Marbletown Rochester and other Patented Lands to the Southward. . . ." Along the way he set sixteen monuments with the eighth described in his notes as "on a Chestnut Ridge full of Large Chestnut timber at the North Side of Shocen Mountain a large heap of Stones Round a Chestnut tree and Marked the tree with N8."

In the early 1960s I visited that corner while running the line between the Hardenburgh Patent and the Marbletown Commons. It was located at the end of the long easterly ridge of Shokan High Point overlooking the deep, rocky gorge known as The Wagon Path between it and Low Point with a view of Ashokan Reservoir off to the northeast. I described it on my map of the survey as "stone on end and stones around, on edge of high ledge on West side of deep hollow called the Wagon Path, on line between the Patents of Hardenburgh and Marbletown, Ancient Monument."

Some years later (in 1988) while preparing a slide/lecture on the history of the Hardenburgh Patent, I decided a slide of this venerable artifact would fit in quite nicely. I followed an old track up the hollow, found a route up the ledge and made my way along the top to the location of the corner. It was no longer there. I recognized my surroundings and knew I was in the right place but the corner was gone.

I looked around the immediate area and was struck by the fact that it was empty of stones which was certainly an unusual circumstance for the Catskills where stones are the principal crop of the land. It then came to me where the stones of the corner and all the others had gone. I peered over the edge of the ledge; Ebeneezer Wooster's corner lay amongst the great number of stones strewn along the bottom.

Some will say the bulldozer and chain saw are simply instruments of growth and vandals are a fact of life and that we must expect some relics from the past to fade away as the road to tomorrow is opened. Maybe so for some things but not for property corners. I certainly can't be characterized as a bible thumper but like all surveyors I hold a few verses near and dear to the heart of my profession. Here are a couple.

Thou shalt not remove thy neighbor's landmark, which they of old time have set. . . . (Deut. 19:14)

Cursed be he that removeth his neighbor's landmark. And all the people shall say, Amen. (Deut. 27:17)

LAUREL, SNAKES, AND YELLOW JACKETS

THOSE WHO KNOW ABOUT SUCH things will recognize the above title as the lead-in to a horror story.

It promised to be a straightforward survey even if the geometry was more than a little out of the ordinary. The 250-acre property ran nearly 3 miles northwest/southeast but was only 500 feet wide on the north and 1000 feet on the south. Just getting to it presented a bit of a problem since it didn't front on any road, public or otherwise, accessible by vehicle. However, we could drive within 300 feet of the southerly corner courtesy of an adjoining owner who took pity and gave us the combination to his locked gate and permission to use his parking area. On the other end we could travel up an old public road along the Vernooy Kill to within 750 feet or so of the northerly line. While these points were only 3 miles apart as the crow flies (or the snake slithers, which we found to be a better analogy), the road distance from one to the other was 8 miles.

The research we conducted before going on the ground was productive. The deeds to many adjoiners included metes and bounds descriptions complete with bearings, distances, and calls for piles of stones and other permanent monuments. We located maps of recent (1985 and 1987) surveys of a couple of neighboring properties, the 1933 survey of state-owned land which adjoined on the north, and an 1860 survey of another adjoiner. In addition, we learned that a large (5,000 acres plus) estate property, which had lines common with over half of the boundary of our property, had been surveyed just a few years previously. We hadn't been able to obtain a print of the map of that survey but hoped to find the lines of it marked or monumented on the ground.

Armed with all that data, Bruce and I were confident that day in mid-June when we went to the field. It was hot. The bugs were out in numbers prospecting for fresh blood. Little did we know what else we were in for.

The walk up to the southerly corner—a reinforcing rod set in an old pile of stones—wasn't too bad. We then followed an old, winding, woods road that one of the survey maps indicated crossed our boundary line some distance up the hill and just short of another reinforcing rod/pile of stones. As we climbed we couldn't help but notice the forest growth on both sides of the road was closing in on us.

I never have quite figured out the worth of mountain laurel. The dictionary says it's "an evergreen shrub. . .having leathery, poisonous leaves and clusters of pink or white flowers." Admittedly, those blossoms are eye-catching and smell good when they bloom in June but that's it. Old-time farmers complain laurel is too coarse to feed to the hogs and not big enough for fence posts. Surveyors curse it with a passion. The groping limbs of the pesky shrub intertwine blocking a way through. The serpentine stalk of the plant twists and turns along the ground waiting to snare the unwary. On the other hand, if one does get tripped up it's no big thing because the mesh of the tangled plants cushions a fall before the victim hits the ground.

We left the woods road and thrashed and crashed our way through the laurel and somehow (blind luck mostly) located the pile of stones and rod we were looking for. From this point on, we intended to run a rough compass line expecting to hit the surveyed boundary of the estate property. Bruce went ahead dragging the 100-foot tape while I tended the back end and guided him with my compass.

It was a tough go. The laurel seemed to become thicker the farther we went. After 50 feet or so Bruce was lost from sight. I followed his progress by the sound of his voice—curse words mostly. We picked up the first monument of the estate survey and continued on flagging 100-foot distances as we went. Bruce suddenly appeared. On top of a large rock above the thickness of the laurel he abruptly stopped.

"What the hell is that?"

"What the hell is what?"

"That!" was the only answer I could get. I dropped my end of the tape and worked up to the rock.

"That," Bruce repeated, pointing to the ground on the far side of the rock. "That" was a black rat snake, this one at least 20 feet long. Well, maybe not quite that long, but at least 6 feet. We had been told to watch out for snakes but hadn't realized they grew to such proportions. After eyeing us a minute or two it slithered off at the warp speed characteristic of its kind. Conversely, our pace slowed considerably as Bruce watched where he stepped.

It was a tiring day. The laurel never did thin out even when we slogged through a swamp and climbed a high ledge. We saw no more snakes but knew they were out there keeping track of our progress through their territory.

The next day, well over a mile beyond our point of beginning, we topped the first ridge and right were it was supposed to be was an old pile of stones "on top of Dickabergh Mountain." Some 100 feet short of that and over 80 feet to the left, we found another monument of the estate survey. We dropped down the ridge and, thankfully, into relatively open woods.

As we walked out in the late afternoon, I realized I was in the lead while Bruce followed. I hadn't paid too much attention to that shift in positions when we headed back down the line the day before but now wondered about it.

"How come I'm out front instead of you?"

His answer made sense—from his standpoint anyway. "If we run into any snakes, it's better you see them first." Well, I guess, but the logic seemed a little one-sided.

We convinced another pair to brush out our flagged line. For some reason, we neglected to tell them about the laurel, the snakes, and the swamp and they let us know about that oversight when next we saw them. Bruce and I went up the Vernooy Kill road heading for the northwest corner of the property. This was marked, according to the old deeds, by "a pile of stones on top of a high ridge of rocks." We found it just as described and, curiously, another monument of the estate survey some 200 feet beyond and below the ledge and 80 feet off to the left.

Over the next couple of days we ran southeasterly from the "high ridge of rocks" back to the corner "on top of Dickabergh Mountain" picking up another "very old pile of stones" on the way. We also found a string of monuments of the estate survey, each off our line nearly 90 feet to the southwest. I was perplexed by the variance between the two surveys and, when next in the office, called the principal of the firm that had conducted the estate survey hoping to get his rationale for putting the line where he did. I didn't get very far. After explaining that we had recovered a number of original corners fitting the descriptions set out in the old deeds, his retort pretty much closed the conversation—"What are you doing looking up deeds? Surveyors don't look up deeds. Lawyers and title searchers do that."

Well, there you go. As the old saying puts it, "You learn something new every day." During all those hours spent over the years in county buildings looking up deeds, wills, mortgages, etc. I had been trespassing on the turf of others and was too dumb to know it. However, I came to one conclusion, I no longer worried when we didn't agree with the estate survey.

We moved next to the long northeast line. The snakes followed us. Or, maybe it was another community of them. Whichever, they were there. So was the laurel. We swore at both and then ran into another hazard.

The yellow jackets that lodge in the ground wait in ambush appearing only when someone treads near their nests or—even worse—steps on them. Then they boil out of the ground and furiously assail the trespasser before he knows what's happening. Those not under attack don't realize what's going on until the victim tears off through the woods swatting his cap at unseen, mad, flying insects. It's all quite hilarious until those doing the laughing are beset themselves. We must have been in the right place, or it was the right season or the right something because we regularly ran into nests of yellow jackets on an hourly basis. After a few of these encounters, I found myself out ahead again while the others lagged behind.

This line proved easier than its counterpart. The laurel didn't seem nearly as thick. Maybe that was because we added one and, then, two young lads to the crew. We found a number of old corners, all fitting deed distances and descriptions. We had this line cold. Well, it wasn't really cold; it was, in fact, hot and then hotter as the calendar moved through July. We rued those cool days of spring we had spent looking up deeds in the county record room, research I now knew was the province of others more qualified than mere surveyors.

Probably the worst days of all were when we returned to clear, blaze, and paint the final lines. We stationed a vehicle in each valley leaving one behind while we worked toward the one farthest away. We couldn't quit halfway through; we had to keep going until we reached transportation. Those were long days but we persevered.

I never went back to the property. I can think of no purpose to be served by going. I suppose the laurel, snakes, and yellow jackets are still there. All that's reason enough to stay away.

I still do my own deed research. Surprisingly, none of the lawyers and title searchers in the various record rooms I frequent try to throw me out when I show up in their exclusive domain. Maybe they're just humoring this old surveyor.

SAMSON

LAND SURVEYORS—especially those who climb the high hills and roam the back country—are a privileged lot; privileged because they see places others don't, become part of the wonder of the changing seasons, and, like Dr. Dolittle, get to talk to the animals.

My client that day was a not-for-profit organization that owned and managed a 6,000-acre preserve open to the public on a membership or fee basis. When word came that a logger was about to commence operation on the adjoining property, the preserve folks wanted to be sure the common boundary line was marked so tree cutters wouldn't stray across it. Armed with the map of a 1940 survey done for a previous owner, I headed up the ridge, sure the boundary could be easily located leaving me with nothing to do except put fresh blazes on some of the line trees marked by the earlier surveyor.

It turned out to be a frustrating day. I wandered hither and yon along the ridge where the map said the line should be, but saw no sign of it. It was hot, too hot for the time of year. The black flies were out, and chewing. My feet were wet from wading a stream running high with spring rains. Worse yet, I hadn't brought a lunch or anything cold to drink thinking I would be out of the woods and back to my vehicle by noon. At mid-afternoon I was still a fair distance from the bottom of the ridge.

When I came to the cooling shade of a small grove of hemlocks, I decided it was time for a rest. I picked out a flat rock that offered a convenient seat. I filled my pipe and lit it, half-expecting some of those no-smoking paragons to suddenly appear from behind one of the hemlocks ready to haul me, a no-account sinner in their eyes, off to the gibbet. About then, if they had shown up I would have told them in no uncertain terms what I thought of some of their righteous notions.

The clouds of smoke I blew into the air soon dispersed the black flies and the afternoon took on a rosier hue. A small stream bubbled with cool refreshment from a spring under a large rock off to my right and reflected the sparkle of sunshine that filtered down through the trees. Woodland flowers with names unknown to me colored the landscape all around.

I then noticed a ring of stones in a little grassy area beyond the hemlocks off to the left. A fireplace, I thought. But, no, it wasn't that; the stones weren't big enough. And they weren't laid in a circle either. Instead, they were set in kind of an oval shape, a couple of feet across the narrower part and about three feet the other way. They had been carefully selected, all were nearly the same size, round, and about as big as a soft ball. The grass had grown over some and fallen leaves from many years filled the center of the small enclosure.

The stone at one end was different from the others. It was flat and set in the ground, sticking up about six inches, a bit higher than the rest. It looked like a miniature headstone. I got down on my hands and knees and moved the grass and leaves away from the side facing into the circle of stones. Letters had been etched on the face of it; not scratched, but cut into the surface with a chisel and hammer. Someone had spent a lot of time trying to get each letter just right. The result was a little crude, with some letters bigger than others, and a few tilted this way and that, but whoever the stone mason had been, he or she had truly cared about what they were doing. I couldn't make out the words; lichen growth blurred the letters. By tracing each one with the point of my pencil, I finally made them out. The single word on top said simply, "Samson." Underneath were dates "1974-1985." I wondered who or what Samson was or had been.

I then saw more words on the back of the stone. These letters were smaller but made with as much care as those on the front. "A Calico Cat" they read. I was obviously on hallowed ground. I sensed a family here—a mother, a father, and, perhaps, two children, a boy and a girl and, of course, a calico cat. It was a perfect spot for a picnic of a summer's day; it must have been a favorite place for them. And especially for Samson. Maybe when here he had chased squirrels. One chattered from the top of a deadfall on the far side of the spring run telling me, "Yes, that's just what that awful cat did." I wondered where the family was now. The children were probably grown and had moved away; after all, 1985 was years in the past. I wondered if they still came back once in a while. The leaves and grass covering the circle of stones indicated they probably didn't. I was sure, however, they remembered Samson wherever they might be.

I came again to the hemlock grove a couple of weeks later. I had copied the field notes of the earlier surveyor. They tied in physical features near the boundary line—a large pointed rock here, an old woods road there, the distance to the stream (which I had to wade again—we'd had four days of rain since my last visit), and a large oak tree next to a round boulder. With these "tracks" left by my predecessor as a guide, I was sure to locate the line this time around.

I had brought along a shovel and dug a hole back of the little headstone. On my first visit to the site, I had noticed a small pinkster bush growing back of the spring run. It was now in full bloom. I dug it up, being sure to get all the roots and a good measure of the soil and duff around them, and replanted it in the hole by the grave. I tamped down the loose dirt and watered the bush with canteens full dipped from the spring. If Samson's family wasn't able to visit anymore, I wanted him to know he wasn't forgotten.

I found the boundary line. It was right where it was supposed to be. If I had been more thorough in my research in the first place, I wouldn't have had to make two trips. However, I would then have missed the reward of knowing about Samson. In my report to the officials back at the preserve, I didn't include mention of the grave. I didn't think any purpose would be served by telling them about this unauthorized use of one small plot of their vast acreage. I didn't tell them about digging up the pinkster bush either.

TERRORISTS

OVER THE YEARS OF MY CAREER I've been called many things—some complimentary, some not—but never a terrorist. That, however, was before that fateful September 11.

It's not commonly known that New York City's Catskill Aqueduct as it courses its way through and next to lands of the Mohonk Preserve is not entirely on land owned by the city. No matter, even those up at the city offices didn't know it until we "educated" them a few years back. In the early 1900s when New York City was acquiring the strip of land on which to site and build the aqueduct, the negotiator for the then private ownership proved intractable. Adhering to the position of his clients, he refused to sell and couldn't be swayed. The city finally gave up and acquired an easement "to excavate and tunnel and to construct, operate and maintain an aqueduct structure and appurtenances necessary thereto, over, across and under the surface of said premises, and for no other purpose. . . ." As for the private ownership, it retained "free access. . .across the easement to and over land owned by [it] on both sides. . ." with the deed specifically stating "free use of the land included in this easement is retained by. . .[the private ownership]."

Some of the lands with this title devolved to the Mohonk Preserve through a series of deeds. Along with it came the key to the gates that blocked access to the aqueduct from highways and other roads. So it is that the Preserve's rangers and survey team travel the aqueduct in the conduct of their regular duties. However, the lack of a gate key didn't stop others from using and enjoying this long, winding, and clear route through the foothills; hikers, bikers, joggers, dog walkers, hunters, bird watchers, horseback riders, etc. were common sights along the way.

In fact, the only ones rarely seen were city employees patrolling and protecting this important public asset. Over time, maintenance of the above-ground part of the aqueduct became a forgotten item in the city's work program. Fences along the strip sagged from the weight of fallen trees; gates hung askew from disintegrating posts giving travelers easy passage around them; the land grew up to weeds, wild flowers (which did add color to an otherwise bleak landscape), and rampant poison ivy. If it hadn't been for the unauthorized users, the whole thing would have gone completely to seed.

Off and on during the summer of 2001, I worked at the Preserve boundary line along the aqueduct and the adjoining orchard lands off the state highway. Finding the line wasn't a problem; it was variously marked by the decrepit city fence, stone walls, and wire fence. Clearing it out so I could set a transit line along it was another matter. Much of it was overgrown with a combination of multiflora rose and grape and poison ivy vines thick as my arm. It took many swings of my machete aided by some well-chosen words not suitable for mixed company to get through it. Finally it was done, the angles were turned, and one fine, rainy morning in the fall Bob and I set out to chain the line from end to end.

We used the customary approach, driving down the aqueduct through gate after gate till we reached the Preserve lands next to the site where police barracks had been located when the aqueduct was being constructed.

It might be well here to diverge from the subject and describe the vehicle assigned to the Preserve's vintage survey team. It's a 19? (maybe 18?) Suzuki Samurai donated some years ago by a friend of the mountains who felt the few miles left on it could better serve the needs of the Preserve. Like everything near the end of its natural life, it was told off to the survey team. Indeed, it did fit right in with the 1898 K&E transit, the borrowed chain tape, the logarithm tables, and the level rod with half the numbers missing from the face and a decided bow in the upper six feet.

The vehicle has had some rough miles added to the well-over 100,000 on it when the gift was made and has done its job well although a few distinct quirks have developed in the interim. It's kind of fun to estimate the speed we're traveling by watching the road through the holes in the floor boards. The clock on the dashboard gives accurate time even though it can't be set—when daylight saving is in effect, we subtract three hours and add ten minutes and when it's not, subtract two hours before adding the ten minutes. Or is it the other way around? I never can remember which explains why I'm either early or late for lunch and most other appointments. It's marked by some odd brown stains inside and out. These resulted from the head ranger's good-neighborliness of helping successful deer hunters transport their catch back to their own cars. Some of these carcasses, still dripping blood, were loaded on the roof and others were simply heaved in the back seat. Speaking of the roof, it leaks. I can always tell when it has rained during the night because the biggest leak is directly over the driver's seat. For all that, it's a great piece of machinery.

Well, back to the survey. We parked the Samurai off the aqueduct proper in a field of poison ivy not far from the foundation and chimney remains of the old police barracks. The measuring was fairly easy along the cleared line and we soon reached the far end of it. By this time the rain had stopped and sun was out. We were the better part of a mile from the vehicle but close to the highway. I suggested to Bob that he walk out to the highway while I went back to the vehicle and drove around to pick him up.

Soon after we parted, I heard a helicopter circling off in the distance. I put it down as a sprayer working on the orchards. I tried to spot it through the trees but it was too far away. After five minutes or so, it flew off toward the northeast.

In due time, I reached the Samurai and drove down the aqueduct, through the orchard lands, and out to the highway. I picked up Bob and turned around to head back to our headquarters on the mountain. Every other car on the highway passed us which was not unusual because our top speed—even downhill—never gets much past 50 mph. The folks in the cars looked at us with questioning glances. I didn't pay much attention to that either; I always figure they're trying to decide which is the oldest, Bob and I or the Samurai.

I then noticed flashing red lights behind us or, at least, what I thought were flashing lights. It was hard to get a good view through the brown streaks down the back window. I pulled over to let the official force, whoever they might be, get by. They didn't want to get by; they pulled in behind us. Now the passersby gave us even more curious looks and with nods of heads seemed to say they weren't surprised.

We saw it was the New York City Department of Environmental Protection (DEP) police as two uniformed men got out of their van. The lights kept flashing. One officer stood at the ready by the rear tire on the passenger side and took down our license number. The other cautiously approached my side of the vehicle, stopping just short of the door.

I later learned the helicopter had been more DEP law enforcement on a regular patrol of the aqueduct. They had hovered over the parked Samurai trying to identify it or determine if it had been abandoned or not. This was obviously a lost cause seeing that it's pretty much beyond identification and always looks as if it's been—or, at least, should be—abandoned. The airborne officers had then radioed the ground patrol to be on the alert for the vehicle in case it ever reached the highway. Once they had us pulled over and got a close look at what they had, these officers probably decided we had driven all the way from Afghanistan and started our journey long ago. The fact that my finely-honed machete lay in full view on the back seat didn't help much in proving our innocence.

It turned out all right once we explained who we were and what we had been doing on the aqueduct. Nevertheless, we were asked for photo identification and our names were carefully recorded in the officer's notebook.

So that's the story of how Bob and I were terrorists for a day. For all that, it was comforting to know New York City was finally giving some much-needed attention to its water supply system.

SURVEYORS I HAVE KNOWN

THE TITLE TO THIS SECTION should not be read literally. These surveyors—or most of them anyway—are not people I knew in the sense that we practiced our profession as contemporaries.

John Richards, especially, was more than a little before my time. His birth in North Wales on April 13, 1765, and death at Lake George on April 18, 1850, puts him in an era qualifying him as a pioneer. I knew him from seeing his name on the allotments of some of the Adirondack townships and having been one of a crew of three that surveyed and restored his grave in 1960. The facts of his life were not known to me—or to many others for that matter—until his great-great-great grandson and his wife decided to seek out all they could about John and wrote a book detailing the results of their research.

I was a lot closer to Verplanck Colvin, although he also was not of my time. As many of us were planning events to recognize the 1985 centennial of New York State's Forest Preserve, we soon realized this early and monumental conservation milestone might never have come about had Colvin not been around and influenced its happening. This, of course, was only one of his many achievements; his Adirondack Survey and the records of it are the stuff of legends. His office evolved over the years into the Bureau of Land Acquisition within the bureaucratic maze of the New York State Conservation Department. I went to work with that bureau in 1955 and eventually became the chief of it. I sat then, as it were, in Colvin's chair and was custodian of his field books, maps, and other artifacts of his Survey.

Ed West was almost a contemporary. His career overlapped

and enhanced mine; I worked for or with him almost continuous-
ly from 1955 to the day of his death in 1988. Whatever I know that's
right about land surveying I learned from him; what I don't know
is not for lack of effort on his part to teach me. I recall the questions
he asked when I went to his home to be interviewed for a job on
his Catskills survey crew. He wasn't interested in what I knew or
didn't know about surveying; he would take care of that part of
my education. He was more interested in finding out if I would
object to toting a transit and loaded pack basket all day long up
and down mountains, if I minded getting wet in the rain or cold in
the snow, if I had a pair of snowshoes, and most importantly, if I
could type. This was long before field offices had the luxury of sec-
retaries and, when I answered in the affirmative to this last quali-
fication, I was as good as hired.

The legend in the "profile" was a real person but with a name
other than I have used. He had worked for Ed West on his Catskills
crew for a couple of years and it was Ed's stories about him that
form the basis for the piece. However, I did know him, and did follow him around some parcels of land he had surveyed—or tried
to, that is. He was a player in one of the stories in the preceding
section on "People, Places, and Things" although I didn't use his
true name there either.

Loyal Nerdahl was another surveyor I never met; however, for
the eight years prior to this writing it seemed he was with me as I
looked for evidence of his tracks up and down the Shawangunk
ridges and valleys. I was guided along many boundary lines and
to remote corners by the thorough directions he set down in his
field books.

I've never cared for autobiographies. They always seem more
than a little pretentious and to have been written because the subject wasn't important enough to merit a biographer. Those who
feel the same can (and probably should) skip the final piece in this
section.

JOHN RICHARDS, Pioneer Adirondacker

THE NAME JOHN RICHARDS didn't mean much to me in March of 1960 when Bert Winne, Fred Haak, and I—officially the Lake George Shoreline Survey Crew—were sent out to locate and map the site of his grave. Bert and I had spent our early surveying years with the state crew in the Catskills. We could recognize the "tracks" of Henry and Ebeneezer Wooster, Will Cockburn, John B. Davis, and other pioneer surveying icons of the Catskills but John Richards roamed the Adirondacks, that strange mountain range far to the north. Fred's surveying experience had been gained in the southern Adirondacks so he had at least heard of John Richards.

We thought it odd to be diverted from what we had been told was a high-priority and long-term assignment. However, like all field men of the lower echelon, we knew orders coming from those remote ivory towers in Albany weren't always the most sensible, so we just got on with it.

It wasn't that we had to search for the grave; it had been found some years before by a veteran Adirondack surveyor who now held down a desk at the Albany headquarters of the Conservation Department. He told us the general area of the site and, with his directions in hand, it didn't take long to locate it. The grave was perched on a narrow shelf about halfway down a steep bank sloping to East Brook, a winding stream that flowed northerly into Lake George. It was a quiet spot hidden away from the noise and cares of the frenetic world. The headstone was broken into three pieces that lay flat on the ground and were partially covered by wet leaves and a couple of fallen limbs. We scraped away the debris and read the inscription:

JOHN RICHARDS
Died
Apr: 18, 1850
Aged 85 Years
Peace on earth and a quiet bed

are the gifts of a forgiving God:
Who is the saviour of all men.
Trust thou in him for good, amen.

In the days that followed we ran and mapped a traverse from
the grave out to the Old Military Road and along it to Route 9 so
future searchers could more easily find the site. We carried in
cement and sand, hauled water up from East Brook, and built a
rustic base onto which we fitted the three pieces of the headstone.
When it was finished, we somehow knew our mission hadn't been
as silly as it had first seemed. While we still didn't know that much
about John Richards, we realized he was part of the history of our
profession and deserved to be remembered.

In later years, I ended up in that Albany office and sent to the
field more than a few directions that were, no doubt, questioned
by those who had to carry them out. My office held old field books,
original maps, dusty land records, and other archival material of
early Adirondack and Catskill surveyors. Sure enough, some bore
the imprint of John Richards. By then I knew his name was memo-
rialized on the Adirondack Land Map. The allotments of Township
1 & 2 and Township 11 of the Old Military Tract had been laid out
according to Richard's Survey it said. He, Verplanck Colvin, the
Jessups, Lem Merrill, and others of their kind were no longer complete strangers to me. I had even followed a few of their lines in the
North Country and thereby gained respect for the enormity of
their accomplishments, accurately subdividing vast tracts of land
in a trackless wilderness with the primitive instruments of their
time.

John Richards would marvel at today's advanced equipment.
He, like many of us nurtured on Jacob's staffs, cumbersome transits, 1-chain tapes, logarithms, traverse tables, and double meridi-
an distances, would find it difficult to adapt to and trust the electronics now available. He would soon realize, however, that the
ability to measure distances to a thousandth of a foot and angles to
the second and even finer doesn't make a surveyor out of someone
who can't recognize an original corner when he sees one and iden-

tifies an old blaze on a tree as a woodpecker hole. Gone are the days when good judgment made a good surveyor.

Those of us with a foot in the past who yearn for "the good old days" are appalled at the work of some present-day and so-called professionals. The early surveyors, John Richards among them, who were first in the field, would be saddened at what they'd find if they could walk once again in the deep woods of the high country. Boundary lines aren't blazed, original corners are ignored because they don't fit bearings and distances cited in deeds, stone walls are thrown out because they wander instead of running straight, maps are drawn by computers and lack the personal touch of a concerned draftsman. Names of original allotments that subdivided the mountain land are ignored and, in time, will be lost to antiquity, never to appear again. Well, enough of that.

Back in 1960, when I first looked at his headstone, John Richards was just a name. I came to know him during my years in Albany, but only as a surveyor. His personal life and interests outside his profession were unknown. Fortunately, a direct descendant of John's (actually a great-great-great grandson) more than wondered about John and what made up his lifetime and did something about it. His curiosity took him into the remote archives, family annals, and scattered records that led to a biography. Now we know John Richards was a multi-faceted individual with surveying the Adirondacks being only one part of the mix.

John was involved in politics for most of his life. He was Supervisor of the Township of Thurman (Warren County) in the late 1700s and early 1800s and the first supervisor of Johnsburg when that township was set off from Thurman in 1805. He continued in the latter office until 1823 and served in the New York State Assembly during part of that period. He was a Warren County delegate to the New York State Constitutional Convention in 1821 and in 1823 was elected to the Federal House of Representatives where he served two years. In between times, John was Justice of the Peace for the Town of Johnsburg, Judge of the Warren County Court of Common Pleas, and a Sealer of Weights and Measures.

None of this, however, kept him from his survey work or from fathering the twelve children born to him and Sarah, his wife, between 1797 and 1815. While attending to the business of his political offices and far-flung surveys for the town, county, and state he was infrequently home but obviously did drop in now and then. He also stopped off at other places. The biography, substantiated by well-documented research, tells of a dalliance with a lonely widow that resulted in at least one child. He took up with— and may even have married—another widow in Lake George. And what—or who—was it that lured him off to Rhode Island now and then?

For all that, it was John's surveys in the remote world of New York's Adirondack Mountains that stand as his mark on history. In a surveying career that spanned over forty years from 1796 through 1836, he ranged almost the entire reach of the Adirondacks. He surveyed and allotted a number of townships in the Old Military Tract from the Canadian border to the Whiteface Mountain country, being credited with the first ascent of that peak in 1814 and of Big Slide farther to the south in 1812. Way off to the southwest he ran the outbounds of the Moose River Tract in 1820 and there laid out the 158 lots in Township 9. He hit all four corners of the Totten and Crossfield's Purchase—Township 43 in the northwest in 1816, Township 1 at Lake Pleasant between 1812 and 1819, the Gore Around Lake Colden in the northeast in 1833, the gores southeast of Townships 12 and 24 in the 1830s, and lands in between. He laid out the so-called Cedar Point Road from Port Henry on Lake Champlain west to the Black River in the late 1820s.

It is fair to say that till Verplanck Colvin came along in the late 1800s, no other surveyor saw as much of the land allotments of the Adirondacks as did John Richards. Indeed, he is worthy of the appellation "Pioneer Adirondack Surveyor."

VERPLANCK COLVIN, The Adirondack Surveyor

THOSE who revere the high mountains of upper New York State equate the name Verplanck Colvin with the Adirondack Park. Indeed, it was Colvin's persistence that finally moved the legislature to draw a "blue line" around the "Great Forest of Northern New York" and declare the 2.8-million acres inside it to be the Adirondack Park. However, those who can decipher the intricacies of the lines of the patents, tracts, and lots that divide these lands and who recognize the weathered bolts set in drill holes in the rocks of remote mountain summits as remnants of a vast triangulation network know the name to mean something else. Colvin was among the early surveyors who ranged the length and breadth of the Adirondack Mountains and, while others preceded and followed him over the peaks and through the valleys of these northern hills, he is still spoken of as *the* Adirondack surveyor.

Verplanck Colvin was born on January 4, 1847, in Albany (New York) the son of Andrew James Colvin and Margaret Crane Alling. His grandmother was Catherine Verplanck, so his ancestry provided both his given name and surname. His father was then district attorney for Albany County and later became a state senator.

Young Verplanck was educated at home by a private tutor and read for the law in his father's law office. Early on, he became interested in geography and the natural world and wandered the hills and woods of the countryside around Albany accompanied by his boyhood chum, Mills Blake. He plotted maps that traced their routes of travel and drew in the ridges and streams they crossed.

Seeking information about the lands they tramped, Verplanck visited various state offices in Albany and dug into the archives of surveys and patents. Here he ran across similar records pertaining to the Adirondacks and was drawn, more and more, to the north. In May of 1865, he made his first trip to these mountains and visited two villages near the westerly and southerly lines of the great Totten and Crossfield's Purchase that encompassed most of the southeasterly quarter of the Adirondacks. Colvin found many lines of the early patents overlapped or left gores, as if the first sur-

veyors seemed concerned only in the patent or township they had
been sent to lay out and had little or no interest in the work of surveyors in adjoining allotments. The situation clearly called for
someone to sort it out and produce a grand map of the Adirondacks, correctly orienting the patent, township, tract, and lot lines
with the streams, mountains, lakes, and the land itself. The project
became a crusade and Verplanck appointed himself its leader.

In August of 1869, Colvin went to the High Peaks, the region of
4,000-foot summits in the northeast quadrant of the Adirondacks.
He returned in December and again in September of 1870. On this
later trip he climbed Mt. Seward for the purpose of making its
"barometric measurement" because "the height of [it] remained in
doubt." He determined the mountain top to be "4,462 feet above
tide-level, or the sea."

However, the elevation of the summit became secondary once
he got there and saw that "the view hence was magnificent." In
closing his report of the climb and measurement of the mountain
to the New York State Museum of Natural History, Colvin called
"attention to a subject of much importance." That, he said, was the
"Adirondack wilderness [which] contains the springs which are
the sources of our principal rivers, and the feeders of the canals."
These would not last long Colvin warned, if "the chopping and
burning off of vast tracts of forest in the wilderness" were allowed
to continue. Colvin's solution was "the creation of an ADIRON-
DACK PARK or timber preserve. . .these forests should be pre-
served; and for posterity should be set aside, this Adirondack
region, as a park for New York, as is the Yosemite for California
and the Pacific States."

The upshot of that and similar pleas from others was the enact-
ment of an 1872 law which established a Commission of State
Parks to study and make recommendations concerning "the expe-
diency of providing for vesting in the State the title to the timbered
regions" of the Adirondacks. Colvin was appointed one of the
commissioners and promptly chosen secretary by his peers.

The commission's report was submitted a year later. It was
written by Colvin in the same flowery language and depth of

detail that would characterize his later survey reports. The commission recommended (not surprisingly) the creation of a state park in the Adirondacks but that's as far as it got. Like so many other studies and reports of commissions before and after, this one was filed and largely forgotten.

Colvin may not have minded however. By then, he had been charged with a greater undertaking. Continuing his interest in the topography of the Adirondacks and the lines of the land patents, he collected maps of the area and annually explored through the mountains attempting to reconcile the differences he uncovered. It was a life's work, he thought. Up to that point he had accomplished it on his own time and with his own funding. At the urging of friends (or so he said) he applied to the state legislature with the result that another 1872 law provided "For Verplanck Colvin, of Albany, N.Y., ten hundred dollars, to aid in completing a survey of the Adirondack wilderness of New York, and a map thereof."

Although Colvin had other interests over the years and was involved in a number of scientific and engineering organizations, from 1872 to 1900 he devoted most of his time, attention, and money to the Adirondack Mountains and the survey of them. It was a struggle throughout. On an almost annual basis, he fought a recalcitrant legislature for funding to continue the survey. At one point (in the early 1880s), it seemed all was lost when the Office of State Engineer and Surveyor complained to the legislature and Governor Grover Cleveland that Colvin was merely duplicating the work assigned to that office. Colvin prevailed when a special committee appointed by the state assembly found his survey to be of a high order and supported continuation of it.

When not engaged in these battles for funding and support, Colvin personally directed the Adirondack Survey. He was a stern and indefatigable taskmaster. His own reports and other surviving records leave an image of him at the head of the transit line, axmen following, with rodmen, instrumentmen, and chainmen trailing behind. Like a bloodhound, it seems, he ferreted out stone piles and old blazes missed by others. The story goes that he ate on the move and when night fell, even in the snows of early winter, he curled up on the ground where he was, rolled himself around in his long, black, greatcoat, rested his head on his bowler hat, and slept soundly till morning. The crewmen were left to prepare their own camps and meals from provisions brought in along the line by laborers hired locally.

The Adirondack or State Land Survey (as it was also known) had its ups and downs. Its high point may have been in 1883 when "Thirteen survey and signal parties were placed in the field." These included three crews engaged in "(1) Primary Triangulation, (2) Secondary Triangulation and (3) Signal Work" and ten others running boundary lines of the state-owned lands in the ten Adirondack counties. In 1873, Colvin hired "fifty-one generally skillful hunters and trappers . . . as guides and packmen." In 1878, Seneca Ray Stoddard, a renowned photographer and guidebook author was added to the Force to head a photographic division. So-called "Assistants" were placed in charge of the various divisions or crews and it was up to them to see that the on-the-ground work was carried out. The most trusted of these was Mills Blake, Colvin's lifelong friend, who was the only person (other than Colvin himself) employed throughout the entire twenty-eight years of the survey.

It all came to an end in 1900 when Governor Theodore Roosevelt recommended the State Land Survey be placed within the Office of the State Engineer and Surveyor and signed a law that provided "The office of the superintendent of the state land survey is hereby abolished."

Colvin (and Blake) were at loose ends thereafter. They continued to journey into the mountains involved in some sort of surveys and magnetic observatons. Colvin purchased land in the garnet country of the southeastern Adirondacks and directed operaton of mines there between 1903 and 1915. He once proposed building a railroad through the Adirondacks but was plagued by the same old funding problems and it never got beyond the paper stage.

In the winter of 1916-17, Colvin slipped on the ice while running for a trolley and fell, striking his head a hard blow on the pavement. He never recovered from the concussion he suffered and, over the next few years, deteriorated both physically and mentally. When Blake could no longer care for him (neither ever married), Colvin was sent to the hospital and was later transferred to the infirmary where he died on May 28, 1920.

Colvin left behind a number of monuments. The bronze bolts he set along the patent and tract lines of the Adirondacks are a permanent record of his passing. The network of triangles created by similar bolts set in the summit rock of hundreds of Adirondack peaks tie the mountains into neat and accurate bundles. He compiled over 300 fieldbooks and an untold number of maps and sketches that form a massive record of the survey. In 1873, the guides of one field crew, on reaching a remote lake not before known, took the "discoverer's privilege" and named it Lake Colvin. A 4,057-foot summit on the easterly side of Lower Ausable Lake in the northeastern Adirondacks is named Mt. Colvin and the 3,960-foot peak next to it is Blake Mountain.

It may be, however, that Colvin's reports of the survey are the best known of his legacies. The 1872 law that first authorized the survey also required Colvin to "render to the Legislature, within thirty days after the opening of the next annual session thereof, a full report of his explorations and survey." Funding for these reports was hard to come by and more than once Colvin paid for printings of them with his own money. They vary in length and quality but tell a fascinating story of the survey in depth and detail of expression. Many are illustrated with sketches drawn by Colvin himself and include fold-out maps delineating the surveys being described. The later reports include photographs taken by Colvin. Regardless of the length of the reports or the narratives in each of them, they remain a testament to an extraordinary survey and the remarkable man who conceived and directed it.

Some reports cover more than one year—the third one includes the years 1874 through 1878. Some are long—the one for 1896 is in two volumes: the first runs to 617 pages and includes a two-page frontispiece, fifty-three other photographs, thirty-two single-page maps, and seven fold-out maps; the second volume consists of fifteen folded maps. Some are short—the one for 1881 is only five pages long. Some years are missing—the documents of the 1886 legislature include a notation that the Annual Report of the Superintendent of the Adirondack State Land Survey was "directed not to be printed." No record has ever been found of a report for 1897. The legislative documents for 1899 state the Report of the State Land Survey "was not published at all according to Mr. Colvin's statement."

Similarly, the documents for 1898 include the note (for the Report of the State Land Survey) "Never printed" followed by 116 blank pages. However, while that note was true at the time, it is no longer. The original manuscript of that report, typewritten with editing and marginal notes in Colvin's hand, was found in the files and records of the Adirondack Survey then in the care of the Bureau of Real Property of the New York State Department of Environmental Conservation. That manuscript together with a lengthy introduction including a biography of Colvin and a summary of each of his other annual reports was brought to publication in 1989 by The Adirondack Research Center of The Association for the Protection of the Adirondacks, Schenectady, New York.

Verplanck Colvin may no longer climb the Adirondack Mountains, but the tracks left by his traveling through them are still there. The lot, tract, and township lines he laid out so carefully on the ground, the lines he traced so precisely on his maps, the lines of text that comprise the literature of his annual reports, and, especially, the "Blue Line" of the Adirondack Park that now inscribes nearly 6-million acres will, for time immemorial, benefit generations of land surveyors and all others who follow him into these great northern hills and valleys. He was and, indeed, still is The Adirondack Surveyor.

EDWARD G. WEST, Mr. Catskills

AT ONE of the functions recognizing the 1985 centennial of New York State's Forest Preserve, Governor Mario Cuomo dubbed Ed West, "Mr. Catskills." It was the right title for the right person. From the moment of his birth in 1901, in the Greene County hamlet of East Jewett in the shadow of his beloved Blackhead Range, Ed West's heart and soul and, for most of the next eighty-six years, his entire being were in the Catskills. He wore that title with pride but treasured another sobriquet just as much.

This one was bestowed back in the 1950s by a pair of adjoining landowners in the back country of the Catskills. The two had long had an honest dispute over the location of their common back corner and agreed to call Ed in to settle their difference. However it came out, they would accept his determination as the final answer. We began at a known corner at the foot of the mountain and started up. Ed was out front with his hand compass while the two landowners followed, each on what he thought was his side of the line. As was usual and normal, Dan and I trailed behind dragging the chain and keeping tally of the distance as we went. Of course, Ed had done his deed work and other research and knew where he was going.

When we reached the distance Ed said would be about right, he stopped and pointed to an old, mossed-over, scatter of stones nearly hidden by leaves and a fallen limb or two and announced, "There's your corner."

It was obvious the landowners had never before seen the stones or, at least, hadn't recognized them for what they marked. Both nodded in amazement and one said, "Why, you're a regular woods detective."

For years after, Ed chuckled about being a woods detective. He said that and other ancient piles of stones had "character." And so did he. He was dedicated to his work, his community and, most of all, the rocks and rills of his Catskills. He found time to be an active member of the Catskill 3500 Club and the Mountaintop Historical Society; he served for many years on the planning boards of Ulster

County and the Town of Shandaken; he held office in the Mount Tabor Masonic Lodge at Hunter and American Legion Post No. 1627 at Olive; he was trustee of the Board of Onteora Central School and the Shandaken Rural Cemetery Association and director of The Catskill Center for Conservation and Development. But he was a land surveyor first and foremost; his profession was his hobby.

If Ed had a fault, it was his driving. It was an adventure to travel home with him at the end of a long day of running boundary line up and down some remote ridge of the Catskills. He was probably more tired that we younger members of the crew, but he wouldn't let any of us drive. The state car was assigned to him and, therefore, he drove it. He could be depended on to say the same thing when he backed out of our parking spot whether in Kingston at the office or out at the dead end of some town road. "Back up till you hear glass." While we never did hear a crash or a shattering of glass, we always braced ourselves and listened because we knew he meant it—he never looked back once he put the car in reverse.

In those years, he smoked a pipe and we could gauge how tired he was by the angle of its elevation. He held it clinched in his teeth and clamped down on it harder and harder as his head drooped lower and lower over the steering wheel until the pipe stood nearly straight up where it seemed it would burn his nose. When it reached that angle, we knew it was time to suggest that one of us drive. He would sometimes reluctantly agree, but not always.

We never actually ran in the ditch, but we traveled partly on the grass at the roadside more than once. It wasn't that Ed was a bad driver. It was just that he let his mind wander while he looked at the stream we had crossed to better remember a special time when he had fished it or to point to the ridge just ahead and tell the story of a survey he had done on its slopes years ago or to gaze at a mountain peak off in the distance and think about the first time he had climbed it. Once, on Route 28 above Shokan, he suddenly veered to the shoulder of the road and stopped. "See that summit just rising over the ridge up ahead? That's Slide Mountain and this is one of the few places where you can see it from a highway." That was Catskills geography as only Ed West knew it and we got a lesson in it nearly every day.

Ed was a dedicated individual. He never did things halfway. He put every talent he had into the task he was involved with at the moment. His credo was that when someone gave you a day's pay, you owed them a day's work. That led to some uncomfortable days, but we had a debt to somebody and Ed saw that we paid it. We were wet more times than we thought necessary. We never knew what radio station Ed listened to for the day's weather, but the forecast was always that it was going to clear. We would stand by the car in a drizzle watching the dark clouds scudding along overhead.

"The radio says it's going to clear up," Ed would inform us as we looked skeptically at each other. "We'll get on our way." By the time we reached the pile of stones up the mountain at the beginning of the line we were to run that day, we would be wet through and the rain would be coming down harder than when we had started. "Well, you're wet now, you might just as well keep working," Ed would say and we were and we did.

Ed worked forty-eight years for the State of New York Conservation Department. He was a land surveyor of renown, locating boundaries and corners all over the Catskills, in the Adirondacks, and across the state. He was called into Albany in 1960 to be Chief of the Bureau of Land Acquisition and to plan, organize, and direct the Park and Recreation Land Acquisition Bond Act. He saw it through to its conclusion before he retired in 1967. That 1960 program is still viewed as the example of how a bond act should be managed.

However, Ed didn't retire. He just expanded the Saturday surveying business he had operated for years into a six-day-a-week concern. In fact, he worked at it up to and including the day he died.

I've always suspected that Saturday work had more behind it than just the fact Ed so enjoyed surveying he wanted another day of it. He knew state wages were barely enough to keep bread on the table for young crewmen and our growing families. The extra pay check allowed for a few luxuries. Ed knew we needed it and always had our check ready before we left for home each Saturday. It wasn't until I began to do the typing for Ed's business that I learned he didn't charge churches, fire companies, and other civic agencies we surveyed for. "They don't have a lot of money and we owe them something in exchange for the good they do the community," was his answer when I asked why he didn't have me fix a bill for this organization or that one. However, we got our usual check no matter that it came from his own pocket.

Some say Ed West's legacy is the 1960 Bond Act, others say it's the thousands of acres he directly and indirectly added to the Catskill and Adirondack Forest Preserves and other public land holdings across New York State, and still others say it's the many piles of stones (those with character, of course) he built and the hundreds of miles of boundary line he blazed. Well, all are right to a degree; however, Ed's real legacy is the knowledge, wisdom, and sense of integrity and dedication he passed on to generations of young land surveyors which will, in turn, be passed on by them to those who follow.

We, and the Catskills, were poorer when Ed West departed this world in 1988 but we—and the Catskills—are richer because he was once here.

PROFILE OF A LEGEND

HIS NAME wasn't really William T. David, but we'll call him that. His wife called him Will. To his clients, who revered him, he was always Mr. David. I never heard anyone refer to him by the obvious Bill. Land surveyors trying to make sense of his convoluted deed descriptions called him lots of things, some of which might be all right out on the transit line but are not suitable here.

Some of his early years were spent on the crew responsible for surveying the lands of New York State's Catskill Forest Preserve. He didn't endear himself to his coworkers when he decided to make a study of the rate paid to them by the state when they used their personal vehicles on official business. Will (we'll stick with that) thought the few cents per mile they got was inflated and set out to prove it. He kept track of every penny spent on his own car over a one-year period, documented the miles it traveled, factored in the original cost of the car and calculated its depreciation in value. At the end of the year, he totaled his figures, divided one by the other, and came up with a cost per mile that was less than what the state was paying. He took his paperwork up to the officials in Albany, who were, of course, pleased that one of their employees had gone to so much trouble just to save the taxpayers a few dollars. The state reduced its per-mile allowance but, as might be expected, didn't return the savings to the taxpayers.

It's not fair to say Will was then drummed out of public service by his peers because everyone who could confirm or refute that died long ago. For whatever reason, Will left the state crew and struck off on his own.

About that time New York started licensing land surveyors. To recognize those who had long been working in the practice, a provision for grandfathering was instituted. One had only to document his experience (which, as evidenced by his handling of the travel expense business, was something Will was good at) and appear before the licensing board to answer a few questions. Will sailed through the preliminaries which consisted of little more than being asked to embellish the facts included in the work history he had submitted earlier. Things hit a snag when that was over and the real questions came up. The first one put to Will was "How do you find cube root?" What the board was expecting as the answer in this age before computers came along to make it unnecessary for surveyors to think for themselves was simply, "By logarithms." Will knew about cube root but had no knowledge of logarithms, so he didn't become a grandfather.

Not one to give up easily, Will scoured the text books until he found an archaic process to figure cube root longhand. He worked the computation over and over prior to appearing in front of the board at its next session. The board had forgotten all about cube root by this time and raised a question on another subject Will knew little about. Again, he failed to become his own grandpa or whatever.

However, Will was a resilient man. He went back home and started a land surveying business anyway, whether the board liked it or not. He was careful not to be too obvious about he was doing; his letterhead said he was a notary public—which he was—and nothing else.

Will was a one-man operation. He did it all. Conducting his own deed research, he produced thick, official-looking, blue-backed abstracts of title, which he laboriously typed on an old portable that had seen better days. He showed up on the job all by himself driving a vintage Model A—or, maybe it was a Dodge, records and recollections are unclear about that. It was understood beforehand the landowner would constitute the field crew and be required, among other duties, to handle the back end of the chain. Once the field work was completed, Will hauled the old portable out from behind the front seat of the truck, sat down on the running board, propped the typewriter on his knees, and pounded out a deed. Will kept a good supply of forms in the truck—quit claim, warranty, bargain and sale—whatever kind you wanted, Will could provide it. Mortgages too; it didn't matter what, Will was there to serve. After the deed was typed, the seller signed it and Will took the signature as he had every right to. He was, after all, a notary public; his letterhead attested to that. Will then packed up, drove off to the county clerk's office and filed the deed.

It's no wonder Will's clients had so much respect for him. He took care of everything. They didn't have to hire title searchers and lawyers and put up with all the confusion, cost, and delay that entailed. If someone wanted to sell a piece of land, all one had to do was give Will a call and it was over and done with in less than a week. It all spilled over into the courts. Judges began to accept Will's deed descriptions, crudely-drawn maps, and "expert" testimony as gospel. I sat in on a court case when one of the surveyors, using Will's earlier survey of the parcel in question as proof, referred to him as a respected old land surveyor. I wasn't surprised when the judge, who was old enough to have known Will in his active days, nodded his head in the affirmative. Whether he knew it or not, the opposing surveyor lost his case right there.

Will's legacy lives on. The deeds he filed in the clerk's offices are still there. The tracks of the old portable and its worn-out ribbon can't be mistaken; the top half of most capital letters didn't come through. Strike-overs are scattered throughout the text along with a misspelled word here and there. Every bearing in the descriptions is prefaced by "about." The citations of added rights and reservations are classic. In the text of one of Will's deeds in my files, the grantor, should he decide to pasture cattle on his remainder land "shall build and maintain the fence around said premises and keep in repair so as to keep cattle out and off of said premises, and will also close the gate or bars in the fence along the highway when passing through either in or out, when cattle are being pastured so that cattle may not stray through said gate way." Some high-priced lawyer couldn't have written it any better.

The big question remains. Why didn't some licensed land surveyor or attorney do something about Will's illegal practice in all those years he went about it? I asked that of the old-time surveyor I once worked for and his reply was, I suspect, universal. "Will's a good old soul and means well. He has to make a living somehow and doesn't do a lot of harm. What would folks without a lot of money do if he wasn't around when they wanted to sell off a piece of land or give an acre or two to their son or daughter? Don't worry, he won't be around forever."

Maybe, but I'm not so sure about that. Sometimes still when I arrive at a client's house, he will pull out a faded blueprint, yellowed at the folds, and lettered in that distinctive awkward style that faces every direction but up and say, "Here's the survey Mr. David did for my father back in the 50s. If you follow it around, you'll come out all right." After cursing under my breath at this unwelcome development, I think, "Well, yeah, if I can figure out just what it was he did."

LOYAL M. NERDAHL, The Unknown Surveyor

WHEN RESEARCHING FOR A NEW JOB, every surveyor hopes to run across some kind of record left by colleague who had earlier walked the same ground. It is important, of course, that the previous surveyor be worthy of the title—some weren't as many of us have discovered. In the case of Loyal Nerdahl, I need not have worried.

In 1994, when I contracted to reestablish (establish for the first time, in some cases) the boundary lines of the 6,000-acre Mohonk Preserve which adjoined another 2,000 acres once part of the same property, I hadn't heard of Nerdahl. That wasn't surprising; my surveying experience had been gained in the Catskills and around Lake George, with a few forays into the greater Adirondacks and far-off South Carolina. The cliffs, talus, and craggy ridges of the Shawangunks were new territory to me.

The Preserve's archive is massive in all natural fields from weather to flora, from fauna to mineralogy, from bogs to Indian sites, and all things in between. It also included just about everything anyone might want to know about the property which had been amassed, piece by piece, over more than a century. These files held deeds, mortgages, notes of negotiations, etc., and a number of field books kept by an assortment of journeyman practitioners, some skilled and some not. A few seemed to be in a class above the others. These covered just three years; in fact, only the two years and eight months between April 28, 1938, and December 14, 1940. The books were eight in number. The notes therein were clear, complete, legible, easily understood, and meticulously kept. All that, however, didn't guarantee their reliability.

My confidence grew when I looked at other Nerdahl documents. Most impressive was a 4' 7" by 11' 6" map that delineated all the lands then owned by the predecessor to the current Preserve and adjoining resort lands. The map also included some adjacent lands under other ownerships. Each parcel was annotated with the name of the then owner and a number. This sent me to a cabinet of numbered folders holding the deeds describing each parcel and, in some instances, a sketch of the land conveyed.

Still, I wondered what I would find when I tried to transfer the notebook and deed distances, bearings, corner descriptions, and ties to the wide landscape of ridges and valleys. Well, everything was just as Nerdahl said it would be. If his notes said he had set a capped iron pipe at a certain location, there it was. If the notes said he had cut an X in a rock and covered it with a stone or stones, it was rare when I didn't uncover that distinctive X. Other corners were marked by drill holes in rocks or piles of stones. I didn't find them all but those I missed had obviously been lost to road builders, tree cutters, neighbors who didn't like the looks of them, and, now and then, a rock slide or some other natural happenstance. Many corners were tied by directional measurements to tacks driven in notches cut in nearby trees. Some trees had been lost to the ravages of time, but notches on those that remained were still discernible to the practiced eye. Twice I found the actual tacks and that was akin to finding a treasure left behind some fifty years before. Nerdahl's distinct blaze on trees along boundary lines was an inverted V or chevron-shaped mark. Finding these out in the middle of nowhere was like coming upon a piece of history.

The bearings and distances from one corner to another turned out to be as reliable as the descriptions of the corners. More than once when I thought a corner lost, I came at it by turning angles from known points on each side and measuring out the distances in the record. Some were simply buried in the duff and debris of passing years but a little digging found them out. Where a boundary line ran along a stream, Nerdahl had actually traversed the center and cut an X in a rock at each angle point. They are still there but I recommend looking for them in the late summer after the cold mountain waters have warmed a bit.

After a few months of reviewing Nerdahl's records and retracing his "tracks" out on the land—and in the water—I realized I was following a master. Maybe I was helped along by the fact that I used the same vintage K&E transit he had. None of this magical electronic stuff for those of the old school.

Just who was Loyal Melvin Nerdahl, Jr.? Where did he come from? More importantly, where did he go? Sadly, his personal record is not nearly as complete as that of his survey work at Mohonk.

He was born October 16, 1909, at Sharon, North Dakota, which must have been not much more than a bend in the road because I couldn't locate it in my 1983 Rand McNally Atlas or the 1977 and 1995 road atlases published by the same company. He earned a bachelor's degree in civil engineering from North Dakota State College in 1931 and a master's from Cornell University at Ithaca, New York, in 1933.

During the summer of 1930, Nerdahl worked as a student engineer with the U.S. Bureau of Public Roads in, one presumes, North Dakota. In 1931, he spent the summer "surveying and plotting 16 parcels of private property." In the summer of 1932, he worked for a construction company as "Asst. Engr., Bldg. Constr.. . .on lines, elevations and layouts of steel, concrete and masonry construction." Following his degree from Cornell in May of 1933, he worked until November of that year as a "Laborer, on building construction." Throughout his college years (and maybe thereafter), he held the rank of First Lieutenant in the reserve ranks of the Corps of Engineers, U.S. Army.

From November 1933 to July 1937, Nerdahl was with the U.S. Department of the Interior, first as a construction foreman, then as chief of party, assistant project superintendent and, finally, "Project Supt. in responsible charge of planning and estimating construction projects, procuring material, supervising foremen on projects, developing recreation and mineral spa areas at Saratoga Spa State Park, Saratoga Springs, N.Y."

The rèsumè in Nerdahl's personnel file is silent as to his whereabouts between July of 1937 and April of 1938 when he began his tenure at Mohonk. In an early 1940 application for the grade of Associate Member in the American Society of Civil Engineers, he stated that he was "Maintenance Engr., Lake Mohonk Mountain House, in charge of surveying and mapping 7,500-acre estate, preparing plans and estimates for repair of buildings and services and new construction, cost accounting and periodical[sic] reports." Dan Smiley, Jr., Nerdahl's supervisor at Mohonk, endorsed his application to the society by stating Nerdahl did his work "Well" and that both his professional ability and personal character were "good." Based on the evidence of Nerdahl's work that I followed, I do believe Dan could have given him a more ringing endorsement than that.

And that's the end of the record. Other than the fact that his wife, Janet, worked as a waitress at the Mountain House while Loyal was on the survey, the file tells no more. His daughter from California spent a weekend at the House in the fall of 1996. I wrote a few years later seeking information about her father but my letter was returned by the mails.

Although gaps remain in Loyal Nerdahl's personal life, his monumental and written legacy at Mohonk attest to his professional ability and character—both certainly more than just good. I am fortunate to have had the opportunity to follow him up and down the Shawangunk ridges and wade behind him in the cold waters of the Coxing Kill.

A WALK IN THE WOODS

There is a pleasure in the pathless woods. . . . —Lord Byron

Finding that first social security check in the mailbox jolts one to reality. Emotions are mixed, of course. It is encouraging to know this one governmental program works the way it's supposed to when so many others don't. On the other hand, that manila envelope is a grim reminder that it's probably too late to make any lasting career changes or set any long-term goals. It may also prompt one to look back and evaluate the life choices that were made and decide if they were right or wrong even though it's a bit too late to change them.

I'm not all that sure when—or even, if—I made a conscious decision to take to the woods and stay there. Assuming I did, it wasn't until much later when I began to wonder if my passing through had made any improvement over what I had found when

I got there. That time of reflection brought me to the realization that my life and the choices I made were influenced by the times, circumstances, events, and, most importantly, by people.

I grew up on my parents' 100-acre farm (which had come down from my grandparents) in the Catskill Mountains of New York State. Like all such farms in that part of the country, it didn't have much level ground. One walked up, down, or sideways. When walking across the slopes of the hills, it was important to change directions now and then, otherwise the uphill leg would become shorter over time. I often considered how well off we'd be if my father could find a market for the stones I picked from the garden plot and potato ground each spring. To make matters worse, the stones were mostly flat and had to be carried because they wouldn't roll down the hill. It was a hardscrabble existence, but my grandfather said it was good for me. It bred character, he said.

Those were the years of the Great Depression and World War II. We weren't poor, but we surely weren't rich. We didn't want for any of the necessities of life. We had our own milk, butter, eggs, vegetables, fruits, meat, maple sugar, firewood, spring water, and even honey from the occasional bee tree we were able to locate; however, we didn't have the extras some others enjoyed. Whatever we needed, we had only to pluck it from the vine, so to speak, or wait until it came into season. Without knowing it, I was learning that nature would take care of those who treated it with respect.

While wandering the woods looking for strayed young stock, I discovered hidden glens in the forest, sweeping views from open hilltops, springs that bubbled with ice-cold water, ledges that challenged my rock-climbing abilities, and a bewildering variety of trees. Eventually, the lost young stock turned up, usually returning to the barnyard before I did, which perplexed my father who had sent me off to find them hours before. But he tolerated my ventures of discovery and usually didn't scold me for my tardiness.

I was blessed with a childless aunt and uncle who lived next door. In a sense, they adopted me and I spent many happy hours with them. My uncle was a self-made woodsman and tried to teach me the names of the various trees that grew in our woods. He explained why one species favored shaded sites while others sought the sun; which trees grew in wet places and which ones on dry ground; why the whole forest needed dead and decaying trees as the nutrient for new growth that would fill the spaces left by those that fell; and why the maples in the upper sap bush assured that our spring wouldn't run dry.

Although it was hard, I enjoyed much of the labor of the farm—even picking rocks from the garden—mostly because it took me outside and into the far corners of our woods and meadows. Perhaps the work I most looked forward to was during the few weeks that counted down the last of winter and tentatively heralded the coming of spring. It was then the sap began to run in the maples and we literally took to the woods. The first day or two of this time brought together my local uncles and aunts in what my grandfather called a bee. The womenfolk washed the sap buckets and the pans that formed the works of our big, wood-fired, evaporator. The men went into our two bushes—called the lower and the upper based on their distance from the sap house—to tap the trees and hang the buckets.

From then till the end of the short season Lenny, our hired man, and I made numerous trips each day up to the bushes with our team of horses pulling the sleigh that held the huge, round, gathering tank. When it was full we went back to the sap house and dumped the sap into a huge vat from which it slowly ran into and through the pans and baffles of the evaporator. Once fired up, my father kept boiling the sap and drawing off the syrup on a twenty-four-hour basis till the run slowed and the trees budded.

I didn't, however, much care for picking blackberries. My mother was the world's best berry picker. I wasn't and had no intention of becoming one but she insisted I accompany her to the sites of past lumbering operations where the berry bushes grew in tangles. (Insisted isn't quite the right word, but it's close.) It took me so much longer to fill my pail and I seemed always to pick where the briars were the longest and sharpest. Picking blackberries was another character builder, I was told. One should have the same patience in life as in filling berry pails and briars were kind of like the brambles I would encounter once out on my own. Well, I guess, but it did seem I could do something without thinking of the message behind it. For all that, blackberrying was an outside activity, so I put up with it.

My mother encouraged me to question almost everything and to seek out the answers in books. She didn't care what I read as long as I spent some of my spare time reading something. I found the rest of the world in the pages of those books and discovered we weren't all by ourselves up there in the mountains; what we did affected others and what others did influenced our lives. This was never more true than in the days of World War II. Events in Europe and the Pacific took young men and women, too, away from our small village and set those of us left behind to doing strange things. We collected old newspapers, rubber, and tin foil, stood watch at aircraft warning stations, turned off lights and sat in the dark when the air-raid siren blew, and learned how to get along with less because ration stamps wouldn't stretch any further.

During this time I set my first real goal in life, made the first real choice about the road I wanted to travel. As I read about the war in newspapers, books, and magazines, I learned about the U.S. Marine Corps and was fascinated by the stories of courage, tenacity, and camaraderie that took the Marines from island to island across the Pacific. I studied the history of this elite and compact organization. This was for me, I concluded and, when barely into my teens, decided I wanted to be a sergeant of Marines and fight enemies in far-off and exotic places.

The war ended before I was old enough to enlist. However, my mind had been made up. When I reached seventeen and after finishing high school, my mother signed the necessary papers and off I went to the swamps and parade grounds of Parris Island in South Carolina. I knew enough to make my own decision, she said, and if that was it, she wouldn't deny me the opportunity I was so sure I wanted.

It was a big world out there; I saw a lot of it. Another war came along to satisfy my wish to do battle. I stormed ashore at Inchon in

South Korea, went through the streets of Seoul, looked north to Manchuria from the windswept and frozen mountains up near the Chosin Reservoir, and slogged through the mud of spring rains as we fought north and south and north again. It was more than a little scary being shot at, but that year in Korea and the overall four years in the Corps must have built more character and I did make sergeant along the way. I wouldn't trade those days and the people of them for anything.

But times change as do goals and it was soon necessary to set another one. Married a few months before my discharge, I had more responsibilities and needed to settle on something with a future to it. But what? I didn't want to be a farmer tied to animals and the cycle of crops; I wanted to be out from under the rigid schedules that entailed. Dot, who had also grown up on a Catskill Mountain family farm, seconded that decision with no hesitation whatsoever.

I wanted a profession that kept me outside and required me to wander through forests and fields. Off we went, then, to the University of Maine so I could train as a forester. Because of some scheduling problems, I ended up taking a number of classes in surveying, mathematics, and drafting with the engineers. It wasn't long before I knew I had found my niche; I would be a land surveyor. That profession relied on precision, called for judgmental decisions, had a bit of a puzzle or mystery about it, and sent one off into the deep woods and over mountains in all seasons. That was for me.

I still have the field book kept during the outdoor laboratories of the surveying courses. My classmates and I were told off in crews of three which remained together for the year through rudimentary exercises such as pacing and compass drills to a complete transit traverse. I still wonder if Ed Salmon and Dave Trask ended up being land surveyors or went into other professions. We did pretty good work on most of our field problems, but failed completely on others. Our most glaring failure was a level run that went from the gym across the quadrangle to the library and back again. The difference in elevation between the top steps of the two buildings was less than 5 feet but we missed closing back on the gym step by 2.383 feet which the professor noted in red in my book was a "very high error." I've recomputed the readings of that nine-station run many times and always come out with the same error. I expect it was all the fault of some guy named Bates who filled in for Ed Salmon who was out that day. He (Bates) obviously didn't fit in with the competent crew he was assigned to that once. Or, maybe, Bates was a co-ed—we had two in that class, the first in the history of the university—and that's what threw Dave and I off. Whatever, my traverses and level runs are now—fifty years later—more accurate than those first attempts.

With a basic education behind me, Dot and I, now three instead of just us two, returned to the Catskills of our youth where I went to work for the New York State Conservation Department. My position—if it can be called that—was about the lowest of the low. I was a Forest Laborer on Survey and carried the transit, tripod, pack basket, and swung an ax on a four-man crew charged with determining the boundaries of the Catskill Forest Preserve. The Preserve consisted of tracts of land owned by the State of New York scattered in the four Catskill counties of Delaware, Greene, Sullivan, and Ulster. It totaled about 230,000 acres located mostly on mountain tops, in remote valleys, and far off the beaten path. It was (and, fortunately, still is) protected by the state constitution "to be forever kept as wild forest lands." In a word, it was wilderness or well on the way to returning to it under the "forever" ownership of the State of New York.

The land surveyor in charge of the crew had over thirty-five years of state service and had been at least once to every property corner in the Catskills—or, so it seemed after listening to the stories he told. He was as good a wild-land surveyor that ever trod those hills and had his own way of doing things. I was sure he would appreciate all the surveying and other related courses I had taken in college. Instead, he swore and said he would have to "unlearn" all that knowledge and teach me what surveying was really all about. And he did.

We climbed high summits, descended into deep cloves, scrambled up (and down) steep ledges, waded murky swamps, and went places where only other land surveyors had been and they a century before. We were afield in all weather, fair and foul; in the cold of winter we worked on snowshoes, in the heat of summer we battled all sorts of biting insects and stepped carefully in rattlesnake country. We were wet and dry, hot and cold, lost in the fog and in the dark of night at the end of a long day, all in search of lost corners and boundary lines. We followed no roads or trails; our only guides were enigmatic deeds, faded maps, a compass, and distances measured off in chains. It was glorious, but over too soon.

The timing could not have been worse. A few short weeks after Dot and I had purchased (with the help of the bank) our first house in the small village where I grew up, I was transferred to Lake George. This was in the late 1950s in a time when state employees didn't hold the right of veto when it came to where they worked. You either went where you were sent or turned in your ax. We couldn't sell the house that soon after buying it or leave it empty and all move to Lake George, so we took the only option we had. I went north and commuted on weekends while Dot and our two children fended for themselves back in the Catskills. The other two men on the crew were in much the same situation so the three of us rented an apartment, did our own cooking, and even cleaned the place—now and then, that is.

Other than the domestic arrangements, it was—as the chief of the Catskills crew had assured us it would be—good experience and I guess it was. The state owned the land under the waters of Lake George up to the mean low water line. Our task was to lay out that boundary line across every dock, boathouse, crib, wharf, etc. along every foot of shoreline around the lake. It was a great late summer job—we saved the underwater structures till then and spent what was probably an unduly amount of time tying them in and measuring their width, length, and depth. That was also the season of the year when the summer girls lolled on the beaches and sunbathed on the docks. Of course, we three married men were not distracted by sights such as that.

A couple of years later, the state recognized the need to expand its land holdings across the State from Long Island to Niagara Falls but especially in the Adirondacks and Catskills. A bond issue was proposed and passed to provide funds to acquire lands for wilderness, wetlands, multiple use, parks, and almost any outdoor recreational purpose that could be imagined. The old-time land surveyor was called out of his beloved Catskills to Albany to direct this major new program.

Once there, he said he wanted someone with a logical and organized mind to help put together the details of the various processes that would control the way the program functioned; I was asked to go to Albany, too. (Well, asked isn't quite the right word, but it's close.) Sensing my reluctance (It didn't have to be sensed, I made it quite obvious) to leave the wide outdoors for the stuffiness of an overheated, under-air-conditioned office, I was assured it would take only a couple of months to get the program under way and I could then return to the field. I didn't see the field again until I retired some twenty-eight years later. Shows how much bureaucrats are to be trusted.

It did, however, get me out of the weekend commute. Instead I changed over to a daily run of over sixty miles into Albany and the same distance home again. It made for some early-morning departures and long days but I was home on a daily (actually, nightly) basis. Fortunately, as time went on, other state employees living along my route of travel were put in the same situation and we arranged a car pool that did allow all but the driver a chance to catch up on some much-needed sleep. Now and then the driver nodded off too but always recovered in time—those of us in a deeper sleep never knew the difference.

A year or so prior to my transfer to Albany I began to plan on taking the examination for a land surveying license. From that point on, I religiously devoted one hour every day to study in preparation for the test. The Lake George apartment offered the right atmosphere for it; I didn't have much else to do there anyway. I got a rude setback when my application for entrance to the exam was rejected. The reason given by the licensing board was that the

experience (of which six years was then required) another appli-
cant and I had gained while working on the state's survey crews
wasn't of a high enough caliber. This incensed the Director of
Lands and Forests who made a personal visit to the next meeting
of the board in an attempt to convince the members that work of
the state's crews was of the highest order. He succeeded to the
extent that Doug and I were allowed to sit for the exam as a test
case. If we passed, the board would accept experience on the
state's crews as qualifying a candidate for entrance to future exam-
inations. If we failed? Well, we didn't want to think about that. It
put the two of us in an almost untenable situation.

I know I felt the pressure when I sat down in the examination
room that late June morning in 1961 and I'm sure Doug felt the
same. We both passed. My grade was 98%, said by the board when
they called the division director to be the highest mark ever
attained for that examination. That one-hour-per-day study regi-
men of the previous two years paid off in spades.

The bond program was a success. For years afterward, it was
held as the standard against which such programs were judged.
Since no one else in the department had any experience running
such a large land acquisition program, we pretty much wrote our
own systems. They might seem primitive when reviewed in the
current age of computers and other electronic gadgetry, but they
were actually the epitome of efficiency. They got the job done,
whereas today's procedures are a bureaucratic maze with traps set
along the way to trip the unwary. Other states (and even some federal agencies) heard about what we were accomplishing and sent
representatives to look us over. Thus, New York's way of doing
things influenced other similar programs all over the country.

Being somewhat autonomous because of the organizational
circumstances of the time, our bureau (of Land Acquisition),
although an integral part of a division (of Lands and Forests) within the Conservation Department, was the primary and, usually,
final selector of the lands (and waters) that were acquired. We
were guided by the criteria established for each land category as
spelled out in the implementing legislation and this partially insu-

lated us from the pressures of local and state politicians who wanted (or, in some cases, didn't want) certain properties acquired. It is
fortunate that those who staffed the bureau were a dedicated
bunch, many of whom had migrated to it from other agencies
because of their interest in the state lands and future of them. This
is not to say that everyone was always guided by charitable
motives, but the proof of their good works lies more in the quality
of the lands acquired than in the quantity.

A side benefit for me was being sent all over the state to inspect
various land parcels being considered for acquisition. It was soon
evident that all lands, regardless of what they were, had a place in
some grand scheme. The purpose wasn't obvious in some
instances In the beginning of the program, I couldn't quite go
along with spending public monies to acquire a swamp, but I
became convinced of the truth of the old saying, "Under all lies the
land." I believed then—and still do—that some lands serve a higher purpose in public ownership as opposed to the misuse they
might receive in private hands. I guess that's when I began to think
in terms of forever instead of tomorrow—decisions we made
would have a greater impact on future generations than on the one
then walking the earth.

As that program began to wind down (it extended over eight
years), I saw the opportunity to return to the field and raised my
hopes accordingly. Again, however, the choice was not mine.

The Adirondack and Catskill Forest Preserves of New York
State are unique in the nation. Created by law in 1885, they had
been expanded over the years through various land acquisition
programs to a total of over 2.5-million acres of state-owned land in
the Adirondacks and about 250,000 acres in the Catskills. Oddly
enough, management (or non-management) of the Preserves had
been left to the departmental field offices almost from the beginning. The directors and staff of some of these took a conservative
approach to management and others were decidedly liberal. As a
result, what was or wasn't done on, to, or with the Forest Preserve
varied from district to district.

In an attempt to correct the imbalance, a veteran war-horse of a forest ranger was brought into the central office of the Division of Lands and Forests and charged with policy-making for and coordination of the management of these vast public lands. Here was a wilderness man, make no mistake about it. In every decision he made, in every policy he wrote, he came down solidly on the side of wilderness and the perpetuation of it. Some wondered if that's what the higher-ups in the department had expected when he was assigned the job but, to their credit, they left him alone and the Adirondack and Catskill Forest Preserves and the future citizens of New York State were the beneficiaries.

In time, however, he approached retirement and so notified the division director a year prior to the date he planned to pack it in. Showing foresight not usually associated with the public sector, the director decided to bring in someone to understudy the old-time ranger during that final year. There went my hopes for a return to the field; I was, instead, moved into the division office.

It was, however, a grand experience. As it turned out, Clarence and I thought much alike. I had a lot to learn about getting along within the bureaucracy of a higher-level office and, most importantly, how to interact with those private organizations that looked over our shoulders to assure we were doing right by the Forest Preserve. They need not have worried. We were, I think, the only true wilderness believers in the department. We did get to the woods; we scheduled as many field trips as we could get away with and wandered all over the Adirondacks and Catskills. When the year was over and I was left alone, I hoped those outside the department weren't able to discern any change in the way their Forest Preserve was being protected. I really loved that job; but it, too, came to an end.

A new bond issue to provide funding to acquire lands to add to the state's holdings all across the state and in many and varied categories was proposed and then approved by the voters. My land surveyor mentor had retired as chief of the bureau that had run the previous program and I was moved once again without much of a chance to say whether or not I agreed. But I adapted to my new post as chief of a bureau and believe the lands purchased under my direction during that program compare favorably with those acquired with the earlier bond issue.

However, I detected a marked difference in the way we did our work. An administration far different than the ones I had worked under perviously was in power. I never knew why, but trust became a thing of the past. Those in charge in the department and "downtown" moved the authority for decision-making higher up the ladder and beyond the reach of those of us at the bureau level. We (and many others) weren't able to make nearly as many choices as we had years before. Procedures became more complicated and numerous checks and balances were introduced into all systems. It was a frustrating time, but we persisted and did the job the taxpayers expected of us. It was a good job, too, in spite of all the obstacles thrown in our way.

As this bond program was drawing to a close, I was sent to the field—finally. However, I didn't see nearly as much of the forests and mountains as I wanted. My new position was as director of one of the department's nine regional offices. I was headquartered in New Paltz and responsible for the southerly half of the Catskills. This positive aspect was offset by the fact that the region extended south to the northern limits of New York City. Being some distance removed from Albany, I was able to exercise some independence in the way I directed the departmental programs. Many of these were entirely new to me, but I was blessed with a dependable and knowledgeable staff who more than made up for my deficiencies.

Throughout the entire period from my first employment with the state through my tenure in the region, I kept active in my chosen profession. In the early years, the land surveyor in charge of the Catskills crew had a private business which he operated on Saturdays and holidays. He hired those of us on his state crew for this extra part-time employment. After I earned my own license, he, his brother and nephew, who also had licenses, and a couple of others formed an association and continued the business. We were involved in all types of surveys from house lots to subdivisions, from cemeteries to wood lots high in the hills, from highway layouts to vast mountain tracts. It was almost—but not quite—

enough to satisfy my wish to be a woodsman far off the beaten track.

My time in the region was short. Less than two years after arriving there, I was "promoted" back to Albany to the position of Director of the Division of Lands and Forests with the additional title of State Forester. It was a long stretch for that laborer who carried transits up the mountains, but the journey was not without effort and devotion to doing right by the citizens of the State—those who paid my salary, meager though it was in the early years. This new position had its pluses and minuses like all the others. On the postive side, Dot and I (our two children out on their own by this time) moved to Albany. My years of long daily commutes were over. We took an apartment within sight of the office and I walked to work and back home for lunch. On the other side of the ledger, I had to give up the Saturday work. I became a true office person growing stale behind a desk and turning pale from lack of exposure to sunlight.

I was seven years in this last position in the public sector. It wasn't easy. I didn't adapt well as a high-level bureaucrat. It required long hours and abilities that sometimes eluded me. I wasn't good at making budgets and became irritated when funding wasn't provided to carry out the tasks and programs assigned to my division. I rebelled on occasion and refused to implement new programs unless adequate funds were provided along with them. Sometimes I wonder how I lasted all those years. The answer, as had been true before, was that I was supported by a superb staff that I had taken care to shift about, one by one, into positions where they could realize their full potential.

Retirement is, I suppose, everyone's goal. A life of leisure, no cares, no worries, and no one telling you what to do combine to create an objective worth striving for. Sometimes it doesn't work out that way. We moved south to bask in the sun. But the sun was too hot, the climate too humid, and I was bored.

Some years prior to my retirement I sat for the examination for land surveyor licensing in South Carolina where we had purchased a condominium. That state recognized my New York license as satisfying most of its requirements but I did have to take that section of the exam testing the principles, practices, and legal aspects of the profession as applied there. I received South Carolina's license in good order and did do a couple of surveys under it, but I didn't find the flat-land work entirely to my liking.

We lasted less than a year and came back north to the fringe of the Catskills. I went to work with my old mentor on a three-day-per-week basis; I was, after all, retired. He also hadn't been able to deal with idleness and was running a full-time, private, land surveying business. Finally, I was back in the field where I belonged. I carried transits again (they were much heavier than I had remembered them to be); I climbed mountains again (they were higher and steeper than they once were); I waded swamps and rushing streams again (they were colder and deeper than they had been); and I was out in all weather, fair and foul—and it was still glorious.

It was during this time that I undertook and completed the most satisfying survey of my career. It actually began not long after I obtained my license. One fine summer day this landowner, who had been directed to me by the Catskills surveyor, arrived at my home bearing a suitcase. It was filled with deeds, maps, and other official-looking papers that had been accumulated by him, his father, and grandfather. Together they described the total property put together by these three generations. It straddled the line between Delaware and Ulster Counties and extended up a long valley culminating in the cirque created by four of the Catskill high peaks. Could I survey it? he asked. A bit overwhelmed by the prospect but relishing the challenge, I allowed that I could.

As time went on and under no pressure to get the job done, I surveyed some of the more critical lines. After I retired, the landowner wrote suggesting that since I had all this extra time, why didn't I complete the survey. It was a monumental task. The property consisted of 8,455.24 acres when we got it done. Fitting together the parcels described by the 123 deeds was like working a massive jigsaw puzzle. It stretched eight miles up the valley and climbed up and over the summits of high mountains. The final map consisted of fifteen sheets each measuring 2' by 3' at a scale of 400 feet to the inch. One could have papered the wall of a large room with it.

My long-time associate, the Catskills surveyor, died at eight-six years. He worked the last day of his life and, I'm sure, expected to return to the office on the morrow. His profession was his hobby and he indulged them both to the fullest. I stayed another six years with the firm as it continued under the direction of the old surveyor's grand-nephew. I enjoyed the variety of surveys and the problems of them; however, I began to find it more and more difficult to keep up with the young lads and gals who made up the crews assigned to me. The electronics so familiar to them only baffled me. I didn't adapt well to the pace necessary to complete a survey in the shortest time possible in order to meet the timetable of the client; I favored a measured and deliberate approach although I understood the need for speed. After eight years with the firm, I retired again.

Well, not really. I reinvented myself as a land surveyor/consultant and accepted only those clients who needed something less than a full-blown survey and didn't expect it to be done overnight.

One of these clients is a private, not-for-profit organization that counts over 6,000 acres of land ownership reaching up and down the Shawangunk Ridge. The bounds and corners of these lands were generally known but a better sense of exactness was necessary if proper management was to be made of them. Most lines didn't require a survey but could be reproduced on the ground by following the "tracks" of a surveyor who done much work on them back in the late 1930s and early 1940s. While this occupies much of my time, I still travel round and about the four counties of the Catskills.

I set my own pace now. If I want to spend the morning in the field and the rest of the day in the office, I'm under no obligation to do otherwise. I can still swing a mean machete; my traverse lines are measured in chains; the 1898 K&E transit I use can still turn angles to the necessary accuracy; I occasionally locate a lost parcel of land after others have given up; I climb high hills, swelter in the hot sun of late summer dog days, curse at the black flies, jump when a rat snake slithers underfoot, wade murky bogs and cold-water streams, and sit on high ledges to admire the view and look back to where I've been. It's still glorious.

Why go through all this biographical stuff, one might ask? It's simply to illustrate for those who follow that one won't get to make many choices in life or career—at least in the early years. It's also to suggest that a person's ethic, environmental and otherwise, is influenced by surroundings and by the people who are a part of those surroundings.

I don't believe I would have become so deeply attached to mountains, forests, swift-flowing waters, bird song, and distant horizons if I hadn't been born and brought up in the middle of these fabled Catskill Mountains. My first sight over my mother's shoulder as she carried me up the hill to our house when she brought me home from the hospital must have been Packsaddle Mountain rising up just beyond the West Kill. I remember I always wanted to climb it in my toddling years and did when I was eleven.

I don't believe I would have sought out the rocks and rills and quiet spots in the woods if I hadn't grown up amidst the mountains with the ready-made opportunity to explore for such things on my own. I don't believe I would have accepted the long hours and unjust criticism heaped on public employees if I hadn't been introduced to the hard work of a rocky, hillside farm at an early age and during the difficult times of the Depression years.

I don't believe I would have ended up as the state forester if my uncle hadn't patiently introduced the fascination of trees to me. I don't believe I would have become responsible for the nearly 3-million-acre New York State Forest Preserve if I hadn't lived in a place surrounded by the broad reach of it. It was the wonder of what it was all about that prompted me to seek a career with the agency charged with "the care, custody, and control" of it.

While I am fortunate the good Lord set me down in the midst of those folks and nature, I am just as fortunate that He scattered people with a firm environmental ethic in the middle of the paths

I traveled. Would life have brought me where it did if I hadn't tramped the hills and survey lines with the old-time land survey- or? Would I really understand the importance of wilderness if I hadn't learned about it at the side of the master, that war-horse of a ranger? I doubt it on both counts.

Thus, my early years set the foundation for what I would do once on my own. But it was, most of all, good people—most now gone—who laid that foundation and built upon it along the way.

ACKNOWLEDGMENTS

SOME of the preceding essays, articles, chapters, or whatever you want to call them were published elsewhere, a few in slightly altered form and with titles different from those used in this volume. Many were first in a biweekly column entitled "Catskill Pathways" that was carried from 1995 through 2000 in *The Mountain Eagle*, a weekly newspaper with editorial offices in Tannersville, New York. The following listing gives credit for each of those previous printings by noting when and in what publication they appeared.

The Mountain Eagle: "Old Stone Walls," March 12, 1998; "The Farmer and His Wife," January 2, 1997; "Loggers and The Rustic," February 12, 1998; "The Collector," February 27, 1997; "Characters" appeared in two columns, August 15, 1996, and November 7, 1996; "A Summer Day, 1998," September 10, 1998; "A Mink Hollow Spring," Spring 1996 supplement; "The 500-Foot Tape," July 2, 1998; "The Winter Woods," March 14, 1996; "Shooting Polaris," March 26, 1998; "Samson," June 18, 1998.

Professional Surveyor, a monthly periodical with editorial offices at Frederick, Maryland: "The Farmer and His Wife," March 2000; "Loggers and The Rustic," January 2001; "The 500-Foot Tape," September 1998; "Verplanck Colvin, The Adirondack Surveyor," May/June 1991.

"Samson" and "Terrorists" appeared respectively in the Spring 2002 and Fall/Winter 2002 issues of *Shawangunk Watch*, the newsletter of Friends of the Shawangunks, Accord, New York.

"A Spring Day, 1969" was printed in the June 1970 issue of

Appalachia, the journal of the Appalachian Mountain Club, Boston, Massachusetts.

The first part of "John Richards, Pioneer Adirondacker" was included as the Foreword to *1765—Judge John Richards—1850, Historic-Adirondac-Surveyor* by James Henry Richards and Patricia Lewis Richards and published by Richards Studio, Kingston, New York. The latter part was distilled from the pages of that book.

The rememberance of "Edward G. West, Mr. Catskills" was published in the Spring 1988 newsletters of The Catskill Center for Conservation and Development, Arkville, New York, and The Association for the Protection of the Adirondacks, Schenectady, New York.

About the Publisher

PURPLE MOUNTAIN PRESS is a publishing company committed to producing the best books of regional interest as well as bringing back into print significant older works.

For a free catalog, write Purple Mountain Press, Ltd., P.O. Box 309, Fleischmanns, NY 12430-0309; or call 845-254-4062; or fax 845-254-4476; or email purple@catskill.net.

http://www.catskill.net/purple